ROOTS OF SURVIVAL

OTHER TITLES BY JOSEPH BRUCHAC

Dawn Land
Dawn Land Audio Book
Long River
Native Plant Stories
Native Plant Stories Audio Book
Native American Animal Stories
Native American Animal Stories Audio Book
Native American Stories
Native American Stories Audio Book

CO-AUTHORED WITH MICHAEL J. CADUTO

*Keepers of Life: Discovering Plants Through Native American Stories
and Earth Activities for Children*
Keepers of Life Teacher's Guide
*Keepers of the Animals: Native American Stories and Wildlife Activities
for Children*
Keepers of the Animals Teacher's Guide
*Keepers of the Earth: Native American Stories and Environmental
Activities for Children*
Keepers of the Earth Teacher's Guide
Native American Gardening: Stories, Projects and Recipes for Families

ROOTS OF SURVIVAL

Native American Storytelling and the Sacred

JOSEPH BRUCHAC

Fulcrum Publishing
Golden, Colorado

Library of Congress Cataloging-in-Publication Data

Bruchac, Joseph
    Roots of survival : Native American storytelling and the sacred / Joseph Bruchac.
        p.   cm.
    ISBN 1-55591-145-5
    1. Indians of North America—Folklore.   2. Indian mythology—North America.   3.
Indians of North America—Social life and customs.   4. Spiritual life—North America.
5. Human ecology—North America.   I. Title.
E98.F6B917   1996
398'.08997—dc20   96-24992
                                                                                                            CIP

Printed in the United States of America

0 9 8 7 6 5 4 3 2 1

Fulcrum Publishing
350 Indiana Street, Suite 350
Golden, Colorado 80401-5093
(800) 992-2908 • (303) 277-1623

Contents

❋

Acknowledgments   vii
A Note on the Use of Names   viii
Introduction   ix

Part I: Walking between the Worlds

How the Buffalo Came to Feed the People   5

Giving and Taking   7
    Grandfathers   10
    Ndakinna Means "Our Land"   19
    Mizi Newetkamigwezo: "The Families Gathered Together"   26
    As Equal as Earth Is to Sky: The Balanced Roles
       of Native American Men and Women   32
    Speaking Again to the Deer   46
    An Unbroken Circle   52

Part II: Storytelling and the Sacred

Why the People Speak Many Languages   63

Opening the Wind   67
    Storytelling and the Sacred   70
    Digging into Your Heart: Hidden Treasure in
       Native American Stories   100
    Combing the Snakes from Atotarho's Hair:
       Native Stories of Natural Balance and Reconciliation   108
    Seeking Out the Real Roots   117

Part III: Thanking the Birds

Horned Owl Finds a Wife   129

Use Cedar to Greet the Dawn   133
   Thanking the Birds: Native American
      Upbringing and the Natural World   135
   Stealing Horses   144
   Striking the Pole: Observations about Indian Humor   153
   The Way a Medicine Person Sees the World   163

Part IV: Gathering the Bones

Red Hand   173

Waking Up to the Seven Directions   176
   Gathering the Bones   179
   Understanding the Great Mystery   195
   Roots of Survival   202

ACKNOWLEDGMENTS

❋

All of the essays which were previously published have been extensively revised and enlarged. I wish to thank the following publications in which earlier versions of the essays appeared:

Denver Museum of Natural History: "Horned Owl Finds a Wife"

Orion Nature Magazine: "Thanking the Birds"

Parabola: "Combing the Snakes from Atatarho's Hair," "Striking the Pole," "The Storytelling Seasons," "Stealing Horses" and "The People Gathered"

National Storytelling Journal: "Storytelling and the Sacred"

Story Earth: "Understanding the Great Mystery"

Z Miscellaneous: "The Abenaki"

A NOTE ON THE USE OF NAMES

✳

In this manuscript I have used the words *American Indian, Indian, Native American* and *Native* interchangeably. In the minds of the Native peoples of North America themselves, any and all of the four are more or less equally correct and equally inaccurate. (I should note that Canadian Native People do not like to use the words *Native American,* but prefer to be called *Native People* or *Native Nations.*) In fact, most Native people just call themselves *Indians* when talking to both white and Indian people. (There, I just used it, didn't I?) Both of the terms commonly used by writers, *American Indian* and *Native American,* contain the historical imposition of a European's name in them. (Again, there is some disagreement here. Russell Means makes a case for the word *Indian* actually coming not from the Indian subcontinent, but from the words *In Dios,* meaning people living in a sacred way, literally, "In God." Further, there is another argument that *America* is not a corruption of Amerigo Vespucci's name, but of the Mayan word *Amerrikua,* "Land of Four Winds.")

In fact, Native people tend to refer to themselves first according to their own tribal or national identity—as Abenaki, Cherokee, Iroquois, Sioux and so on. Here, too, there are problems. *Iroquois* probably comes from an Abenaki word *Ireokwa,* said to mean "real adder snakes." The Iroquois originally called themselves *Haudenosaunee,* "People of the Longhouse." Such renamings in the languages of their rivals occurred with many Native nations in the five hundred years since Columbus. The Lakota became *Sioux,* the Dineh became *Navajo,* and so on. Now these names are even interchangeably used by many of the re- and misnamed Native nations themselves.

INTRODUCTION

❁

A decade ago, my friend and collaborator Michael J. Caduto and I began the work of creating a series of books which would use traditional Native storytelling to teach science to children. It was our understanding that rather than being "mere myths," with "myth" being used in the pejorative sense of "untruth," those ancient traditional tales were a distillation of the deep knowledge held by the many Native American nations about the workings of the world around them. The success of that series, beginning with *Keepers of the Earth,* which has close to a million copies in print, is not a testimony to our insight, however. It is an affirmation of the strength of those stories, an indication of how much those stories are still needed. It led me to think deeper about the stories and to begin to speak and write about them in different ways.

▲▼▲

Roots of Survival began as a series of essays about various aspects of American Indian storytelling. As it grew into a book, however, it began to take some different directions. We are nearing the end of one of the most violent centuries in recorded history. There is, throughout the world, a climate of deep concern about the impact which human beings have on the earth and all of the life around them. As a storyteller, I've long been aware of the dual purpose of stories in American Indian life—that stories are designed to both entertain and teach. As I've grown older, I've also learned that our stories frequently (if not always) have a third purpose. That purpose is to heal. We human beings are not just body and mind. We are also spirit and emotion. There are few things which speak as clearly as stories speak to the needed balance between all four of those components which make up human life. Stories have great power.

I have also learned that stories may have the power to destroy. If told wrongly, if told with evil intent, stories can confuse the minds and

---

* Michael J. Caduto and Joseph Bruchac, *Keepers of the Earth* (Golden, CO: Fulcrum Publishing, 1988).

the spirits of those who hear them. They can lead the listener away from balance and into the twisting paths of anger. We have all heard such stories. Stories in which those from other cultures are portrayed as evil and dangerous have been used to convince people that those others are less than human and must be eliminated. The power of Hitler's Third Reich was, in part, the power of a destructive myth which was all too well told. Some of the popular stories of the American frontier in which bloodthirsty Indians are killed as if they were vermin or the tales told in the pre–Civil War South of lazy and ignorant African slaves are strikingly similar to the Nazi portrayal of the Jews. Ethnic caricatures and sexist "humor" are further examples of the way certain stories can debase and lessen the humanity of others. In a very real sense, stories can be used to kill both the spirit and the body.

There are many ways to survive. We can do so at the expense of others, at the expense of the natural world and those who are physically weaker. We can do so in an incomplete fashion, surviving physically, but carrying with us a sense of incompleteness, a feeling of being hollow. We can be, as American Indians observed in the eighteenth and nineteenth centuries when they ventured into such great cities as New York and Pittsburgh and saw how inhumanely the people of those cities treated each other, among the "walking dead." Or we can survive as fully human in the American Indian sense. We can be aware of the earth below and the sky above, aware of the beauty all around us and the necessity of walking in balance as we travel.

I think of how the Lakotas who were recruited to be part of Buffalo Bill Cody's Wild West Show at the end of the nineteenth century traveled. When they were performing in New York City and in London they observed the many hungry white children dressed in rags who were begging in the streets. They asked whose children those were and they were told that those children were orphans. They belonged to no one. The Lakotas shook their heads. How can that be? they asked. Don't the *Wasichus,* a Lakota word for the European American which means "those who take all the fat for themselves," realize that all children are their children?

I find myself imagining the conversation that went on then between those men who had fought in the battles of the Little Big Horn and the Greasy Grass. I know that they held in their own memories the old stories of children whose parents died, yet those children were raised by uncles and aunts, by grandparents or other elders. And if there were no people around, those children were adopted by the animals. Moses Big Crow is a contemporary Lakota storyteller whose book, *A Legend of Crazy Horse Clan,* tells of an orphan child raised by the buffalo, a child who became an ancestor of the great leader Crazy Horse. Then, after talking—perhaps after little talk at all—those Lakotas made their decision. The newspapers of the time spoke of that decision, telling how after every show those men—Black Elk, Sitting Bull and the others— would walk out into the streets of New York and London to use all of the money they had been paid to buy food for those hungry white orphans.

I believe that in those old stories and in the more recent stories of those who chart the path of their lives by the directions those ancient tales continue to give us, we can find the real roots of survival. So this book is not just a book about American Indian storytelling. It is itself a story. It tells of my own journey along those well-marked trails. It speaks about the relationships which have been developed over thousands of years between human beings and the world which is both outside us and within us all. There was no word in any American Indian language for "ecology," yet the stories point us again and again to the conclusion that living in ecological balance was the desired goal of most, if not all, Native cultures. Beauty is balance. The Dineh are the people most often called Navajo. In the Dineh language, the word *hozho* contains two meanings—"beauty" and "balance." One well-known part of the great healing chant of the "Beautyway," a chant in which storytelling is used as an integral part of ceremonial healing, is usually translated something like this:

> Beauty before me I walk,
> Beauty behind me I walk,
> Beauty below me I walk,
> Beauty above me I walk,
> Beauty all around me I walk. ...

But the English language allows us to see only one dimension when we choose the word *beauty* alone. Beauty is also balance. It is a crucial distinction. Not only is balance beautiful, things cannot be beautiful unless they are in balance. A man with money cannot be content when children are starving in the street. Even if those children are not biologically his own, they are his own in spirit.

▲▼▲

Long ago in Europe, I believe, something happened. I am not certain how it began, but people began to follow a wrong road. Not all of the people, perhaps, but those who now called themselves the leaders. They followed that road which led away from the awareness that the earth is sacred. It is not apart from the Creator, but a part of Creation. But the further they went down that road, the harder it became for those new leaders to acknowledge or remember that. That road also led away from the power of women, those who bring life into the world and whose lives are intimately connected to the powers of Earth. That road led so far that those women who remained in connection with the old ways became viewed as a threat. Now they were no longer healers and seers, those women were "witches" and condemned to death. No one knows how many were killed. Hundreds of thousands, certainly. Perhaps millions. In a great paroxysm of self-destruction, the new civilizations of Europe diminished and twisted the powers of women and the earth. It may even have wiped out a whole segment of the gene pool of Europe, those who had that deep healing vision. Some, of course, went into the deep woods and the mountains, into the swampy places where pursuit was hard. Some of those people and their old ways survived there.

It was justified in the name of God. Yet if God is as great as we are told, how could that God who created Earth and human beings be threatened by Earth, by women, by healing? That is not my question, but a question asked by many American Indian people who see that stage of European civilization as a time when human beings went crazy. Now the Europeans created new stories, ones as destructive as their old half-forgotten tales of healing and redemption had been. In those new myths of death, old witch women who wanted to eat children lurked at the edges of towns in the evil woods. It is the story of Hansel and Gretel. Animals which had once been seen as brother and sister beings, helpers and guides, became as evil as human fears of them. And this is the story of Little Red Riding Hood. The only way to counter those monsters, human and animal, became to kill them and also extirpate the wild places where they sought refuge. The woods and swamps, the forests and heaths (from which we get the word *heathen*), had to be destroyed.

Now imagine this continent as a place where that did not happen. Imagine a land of many different peoples, none of them perfect. There is occasional warfare, but none of these peoples are at war with themselves and their land in that same way as the peoples of Europe. These people have towns and cities in some places, small settlements of no more than a few families in others. They have learned to make use of the natural world around them in a seasonal round of activities which can be sustained from one generation to the next. Their stories, their songs and ceremonies, remind them of the sacred nature of the world in which they live. Imagine the coming into this world of that first recorded emissary of the European way. Imagine Columbus.

▲▼▲

Ironically—or perhaps understandably—many Europeans immediately sided with the Native peoples. We hear of the conquest of Mexico by Cortés, but we do not hear of the Spanish castaways on the coast of Mexico who arrived before Cortés and were taken in by the Mayan people. One of those white men even helped his new adopted relatives build fortifications against the invasion he knew would eventually come. We hear of the Mayflower Colony, but we seldom hear of the strict laws that had to be passed there to keep white men and women from "Going Native." It was not that Indian life offered something new and different. It was that people wanted to return to the old way. (My own family is of mixed Indian and European descent. My sister, Margaret, once asked our Slovak grandfather why he never went to the Catholic Church. All of our Slovak relatives appeared to be devout Catholics, yet he seldom set foot in the Greenfield Catholic Church. "I worship," he said to her, "in the old way. In the forest, with the trees.")

Despite centuries of living at war with all the rest of life on this planet, living in a culture so divided that women had become property, many European men and women kept somewhere within them a memory of what it was to be fully human. If we read the "Captivity Narratives" of the seventeenth and eighteenth centuries, those stories of white men and women, boys and girls, who were taken prisoner by the Indians, we find a curious consistency in them. The longer those Europeans (of any age) lived with the Indians, the more they identified with them. Eventually, they no longer considered themselves white and they refused repatriation, preferring to live out their lives as Indians.

The tendency of non-Indians (including escaped African slaves who quickly found acceptance and common cause with Indians) to "Go Indian" was one of the earliest problems for Western civilization in the Americas. It is, I feel, still a problem to this day. If Earth is viewed as sacred or to be owned in common, that is a great threat to developers at all levels—from real estate agents to multinational corporations. It is no accident that policies of environmental protection, clean air and water standards, national parks and protected lands such as those of Alaska came under attack in 1995 from a Congress controlled by white men whose imperatives are much the same as those who destroyed the once-sacred lands of Europe long ago. That Indian values, such as caring for children and the elderly, and Indians themselves were attacked with equal energy by that same Congress should have been taken for granted. The Indian wars are still being fought for the soul of the land.

▲▼▲

Many Indians, I might add, feel that "Going Indian" is sometimes a problem for Indians as well. The eagerness of whites to "become Indian" when they have no idea what that really means can be a source of embarrassment and misunderstanding. I am not a Mason and I would never dream of walking, without an invitation, into a Masonic Temple when a meeting is being held. Yet non-Indians have so frequently intruded, uninvited, upon Indian ceremonies that in many parts of North America, Native communities now have rules requiring all non-Indians to leave before sunset.

Part of this is due to the impatience which seems to characterize modern American life. People want things right now, with no waiting period. The dominance in the Western world of clocks and the measuring of human activities in terms of "time" (with time equated as money) is something I'll deal with in a later essay. I recall a person who approached me while I was selling books at a powwow.

"How can I learn about Indian medicine?" that non-Indian said.

"I could suggest some books for you to look at."

"No, I want to learn directly from an Indian medicine person."

I took a deep breath. Be polite, I reminded myself.

"If you have a sincere interest in learning from a medicine person, it will take years. You have to devote yourself to it for a long, long time. You really have to be accepted into that person's family and take on the responsibilities of being like a family member," I said. But the person to whom I was talking was already shaking her head.

"No," she said, "I was thinking of something more along the lines of a weekend seminar."

"Life," I said, "is not a weekend seminar."

▲▼▲

In that same vein, let me say that this book is only that. It is a book about stories, American Indian storytelling and the spirit surrounding storytelling and our place on this planet. It is only one step along that way and it is no substitute for the actual journey. Yet I hope that, as books sometimes do, it may lead some to set forth on the real roads. And to those who do, I offer this parting word we speak in Abenaki, a language which has no word for good-bye. *Wlipamkaani.* "Good traveling."

ROOTS OF SURVIVAL

PART I

WALKING BETWEEN THE WORLDS

How the Buffalo Came to Feed the People

(A Kiowa Story)

Saynday was coming along and when he came to a village he heard the people talking.

"We are hungry," the people said. "We would be thankful if we had animals to hunt so that we could have meat, but White Raven owns all the animals. He and his family are fat and happy while we are starving."

"This is not right," Saynday said. He turned himself into a fuzzy little puppy and went to White Raven's lodge. He walked into the lodge, went right over to White Raven's daughter and rolled over on his back at her feet.

As soon as White Raven's daughter saw him she said to her father, "I want to keep this puppy."

White Raven was suspicious. "That puppy looks strange," he said. "You cannot keep it."

But White Raven's daughter was used to having things her own way. She begged and cried and at last her father gave in. That night, when it was time to prepare food, Saynday, the puppy, watched as White Raven left the lodge and went to a big black stone. He rolled it aside and went down into a hole in the ground. He was gone a long time and when he came back out, he was carrying fresh buffalo meat.

"Hah," Saynday thought, "this is interesting."

The next day, White Raven and his wife got up early. "We have to travel today," they said to their daughter.

"I don't want to go," she said. "I want to stay and play with my puppy."

"You may do so," said White Raven. "But do not show him where we get our meat." Then White Raven and his wife left.

That day, as White Raven's daughter played outside with her

puppy Saynday, she kept trying to play with him near the big black stone. But every time she came close to it, Saynday the puppy would run away. She tried calling him over to the stone, but Saynday ran in the other direction. At last, the daughter became angry. She picked Saynday up and carried him over to the stone.

"You silly puppy," she said. "Do not be afraid of this stone. It is where we keep our meat. I will show you." Then she pushed the stone aside.

As soon as she did so, Saynday jumped down into the hole under the earth. He looked around. All around him were buffalo, big ones and small ones, bulls and cows and calves. He began to run around and bark at them and the buffalo began to run. They ran right up out of the hole and onto the plains. White Raven's daughter tried to stop them, but it was too late. All of the other game animals who had been kept in the hole with the buffalo came running out behind them—the elk and the deer and the antelope all came out onto the plains, too, as Saynday chased them.

White Raven and his wife heard the sound of the animals' hooves and came running, but the herds of animals ran right past them. Saynday turned himself into a burr and stuck to the leg of the last buffalo and was carried past without White Raven seeing him.

When they were far out on the plains, Saynday changed back into his own shape and spoke to the buffalo.

"This is where you will always live now," he said. "You will not live underground. You will have all this green grass to eat and all of this land to roam around on. No one person can own all the animals. Now if people wish to have meat they must hunt for you, but they must always show you respect and give thanks for the gift of the food they are given. They must share and not take too much. If they do not treat you in the right way, do not allow them to catch you."

So it was and so it is to this day.

Giving and Taking

Life is a circle. Those who have been given something, whether physical ability or knowledge, must return their gift to the community by sharing. That kind of giving is neither giving up nor losing, for it makes the individual and the circle stronger. Harold Tantaquidgeon, a Mohegan elder, explained it to me as a circle divided into four parts symbolizing the stages of life and the process of gaining wisdom. *Listen, Observe, Remember* and *Share.* That, ideally, is how it was in the many Native communities of this hemisphere.

What makes it all so complex now is that, as the Lakota leader Sitting Bull said, there are no longer just Indians here. That multisocietal complexity is one reason why we must teach each other. Understanding can bring respect. So, Native people continue to share, even using such new ways as books and audiotapes, videos and CDs. Yet contemporary Native Americans are surrounded by non-Natives eager for the kinds of community and knowledge that characterize Native life at its best. Some are as hungry for the wisdom and spiritual traditions of Native people as others were in the past for Native land. Instead of accepting the gift and the responsibility which goes with it, they think wisdom can be bought or taken. But real wisdom can only be given and shared. It becomes the opposite of wisdom when it is wrongly taken and selfishly used. The job of the Native writer and the publisher of Native American books is to be part of that sharing, part of that gift. What is sold is only paper and ink and an individual's way of presenting that wisdom. What is truly given is knowledge that must be respected, knowledge meant to be shared.

Think, then, of any gift of knowledge whether it is words found in this book or a teaching given you through the living breath as part of that sharing. Think, too, of the responsibility which we accept when we accept such a gift. Think of balance.

I was told, back when I first began to learn a little about medicine plants, that unless we are in the right frame of mind when we go to gather medicine, the medicine plants will hide from us. When we pick them, we must do so out of personal need—a need for the health of our own bodies or the health of someone we wish to help. Again, if we do not do this out of true personal need, the plants will not allow themselves to be found. Even then, after we have found those plants, there are certain rules to be observed. Because plants grow together in families, we must never take the largest plant in that group. We must leave it so that it can continue to lead its family, to bring new generations into the world.

Sadly, the medicine plants do not always hide from those who seek them for the wrong reasons. The novels of Carlos Castaneda, beginning with *The Teachings of Don Juan: A Yaqui Way of Knowledge,* have very little connection with the real lives and traditional practices of any Native American peoples, much less the Yaquis. All of the books of Castaneda appear to be—as Richard de Mille concluded in his 1976 book *Castaneda's Journey* (Capra Press)—a blend of fantasy and plagiarism. Anyone who tries to follow their teachings is taking the same risk that the ducks took in one of the stories of Manabozho, the trickster hero of the Anishinabe.

"Come into my lodge and let me teach you a new dance," Manabozho said to the ducks.

They didn't notice the hungry gleam in his eye. They went into his lodge. A big fire was burning in the center.

"Now dance around in a circle. Keep your eyes closed or the smoke will make them red. I'll beat my drum and sing. You dance and keep dancing till I tell you to stop."

Then Manabozho began to sing loudly and play his drum. The ducks danced with their eyes closed. As they danced, Manabozho sang louder and louder. He sang so loudly that the ducks could not hear the sound of Manabozho grabbing them one by one and wringing their necks.

Yet Castaneda's writings about the use of the peyote cactus has led to the gathering of those cactuses by the thousands. People use peyote recreationally—to take a trip. But it takes decades for a small peyote cactus to reach maturity. As a result, that plant which is used sacramentally in the Native American church has become rare or even wiped out in much of its original range.

▲▼▲

When you take, it is your responsibility to give back in equal measure. When gathering medicine plants, you are supposed to say thank you and place a small gift—perhaps a little tobacco—there on the earth. If that plant gathered has seeds, you are supposed to loosen the soil and plant some of the seeds from the plants you picked. Doing this not only helps the plants, it also reminds you where you truly are. It seems as if very few people are able to be where they are these days. The saying "wherever you go, there you are" is being replaced by "wherever you go, there you were."

Listen, then. Listen to your own heart beating. Listen to the sounds your feet make on the earth. This earth is a drum. Are you playing the right tune?

Observe. Look at the place you stand. What holds you up and what are you standing on or walking over? I was told by my old friend Swift Eagle that his Apache people were taught to pass through the way a fish swims through the river, leaving little changed by their passing. Only a ripple in the water.

Remember. What have you been given? Who gave it to you? Where are the places that you have been, and when you began this journey, where did you think you were going?

Share. Simply share. The earth is a gift. We can never give back as much as we are given and so we must spend our lives giving.

> Snow falls,
> covers earth.
>
> Our feet leave tracks—
> not of where we are,
> but where
> we thought we were.

GRANDFATHERS

✦

One day in late June, the time of year many of the Native people of the East Coast always called the Moon of Wild Strawberries, I was on an airplane flying from Chicago to Albany, New York. In that place between Earth and Sky, between sleep and waking, between the roar of the engines and the soft whispering of the clouds, I found myself drifting. I was sad, but not afraid. I'm never afraid on airplanes, just as I never seem to have stage fright before I do a poetry reading or a storytelling performance or a lecture before an audience. Perhaps it is because I have this feeling that I'm not alone as I do these things, as I fly or speak or sing. I remember, almost a quarter of a century ago when I was teaching in West Africa, first recognizing that feeling of not being alone, of feeling a familiar and comforting presence. I could not give that presence a name then, but I can now. *Grandfather.* An old name. A presence that has grown stronger as I have grown older, as those elderly people whose lives and words have blessed me, have chosen to walk to the top of that hill which rises between those who continue to breathe the winds we know and those who have chosen to go with the breath of the spirit and join their own old ones who went before them. *Grandfather.* It is a word with more than one meaning for Native people.

When I say that word I think of The Thunders, the old strong ones whose voice we hear in the storm. *Bedagiak* is their name in the Abenaki language spoken three generations ago by one branch of my family. They are the Grandfathers who use their spears of lightning to destroy monsters. In 1989 I was doing a poetry reading in Germany. Suddenly there was a sudden earth-shaking clap of thunder. It shook the building and the people in the audience looked up apprehensively. "Grandfather," I said, "it is good to hear you in this land, too." Several of the people in the audience told me after the reading how much they appreciated my saying those words because it changed the whole mood. Though they'd been startled and made nervous by the thunder, my greeting to it made them relaxed again. Yet I only spoke that word because it was the right word to say. *Grandfather.*

And when I say that word I think also of the man who raised me, the Abenaki man who was my mother's father. He was quiet, even guarded about his Indian blood—though one only had to look at him to see who his ancestors were. His ways of teaching me were ways which used few, if any, words. One of my earliest memories is of the time I climbed the ladder with him. I do not know now if it is a memory which I remember, or if I only remember others' telling of it so well that it has become a part of me. I was only three years old. I have a picture of the two of us then. My Grandfather, his face darker than a single generation of sun could make it, leans slightly to hold the left hand (the hand closest to the heart) of a very small boy with a serious face. Both the old man and the boy are looking ahead and slightly to the right, as if seeing not the camera, but what is beyond it, a difficult world to walk through, and a world where a child is safest when his hand is held by an elder who has been that way before.

Perhaps because of his Indian blood, perhaps just because of the way his Abenaki Basket Maker parents raised him—never shouting at him, never striking him, never discouraging him from trying things which were difficult or dangerous—my Grandfather was unafraid of heights. Even in his eighties, he would still place the extension ladder up against the tall house, and climb up to walk the peak of the roof, pausing to look toward the southeast where the morning sun touched the edge of the hills and glittered bright as quicksilver off the lake called Saratoga.

That day of my memory, he had climbed up to look at something on the roof. Perhaps he forgot, for a moment, that I was his shadow, always close behind him. Or perhaps he thought the rungs of the ladder too high for me to reach. But a sound made him turn and look and see me there, at the top of the ladder, looking around, thirty feet above the ground. Another man might have shouted or grabbed at a child in such a dangerous place. But my Grandfather only said, "Forgot something. Got to go back down. You go first, Sonny." And I went down the ladder, my Grandfather close behind. I was a little confused when we got down, though. My Grandfather didn't go get whatever it was that he had forgotten to bring up there with him. Instead, he just took down the ladder and then sat there for a long time with his arm around me, not saying anything.

My mother was with me in the hospital on the day my Grandfather died. It was six months after my wife and I and our year-old son had returned from Africa, to come back to him and the house where I was raised, the house where I have raised my own two boys. Though sick, he'd waited for us to return, kept the house for us, tended the council fire. And now he was tired. He smiled at us, his only daughter and the child that he and his wife had taken from her to raise as his son, and said, "You go ahead and go home. I'm going to bed now."

My mother didn't understand. "But Pop," she said, "you're already in bed."

"I know where I am," my Grandfather said. "I'm going to rest now. Don't you worry about me."

We left the room and before the elevator had reached the bottom floor, his spirit had left his body. And though I cried, I knew he wasn't gone. Those who have died, my Iroquois teachers say, are no further than the other side of a leaf which has fallen.

▲▼▲

The late Senegalese poet, Léopold Sédar Senghor, wrote in one of his poems that he always confuses life and death, that the two are joined by a tender bridge. It is that confusion between those two worlds or, for Senghor's words are tinged with gentle irony, that understanding of the connection between them which is so missing in the lives of the majority of Americans today, including many of our poets. It is, I think, one of the reasons why so frequently contemporary poetry is a poetry of self-centeredness, of alienation, of unredeemable loss and cynicism.

Yet that cannot be said of much of the poetry and other writing being produced by Native American writers, by writers like myself whose lives have been deeply affected by their connection with another way of saying and seeing the world, a gentler yet no less tough vision of reality. Those who recognize that we are always walking between the worlds which European traditions describe as reality and fantasy, as sacred and profane, as natural and supernatural, as life and death, are not immune to pain and suffering, to error and confusion, but they do tend to recognize more clearly what state, what world they are in; their words and their lives seek a balance which others—including all too many politicians and teachers, clergy and corporate heads—either cannot see or refuse to perceive. Those others, whose ears and eyes are closed, cannot believe that everything around them is sacred. They cannot see the connection. But when our ears and our hearts are open, we hear things which have always been there—like the background hum of fluorescent lights in an office building or the soft drone of insects on a summer night or the wind through the grass of the prairies whispering just as the sun breaks the edge of the world and makes the shadows run across the land. As it did one June morning when my Cheyenne brother-friend Lance Henson and I stood on top of King Mountain in southwestern Oklahoma and dropped the dried needles of cedar on top of the embers of our fire, so that the twenty young people, Indian and non-Indian alike, who had followed us up that mountain in the dark could wash their hands and faces—and hearts—with that cleansing ancient smoke.

When the sun was a hand's width above the horizon, we led our small group to a place that Lance and I had found the day before. It was an indentation in the stone of the mountaintop just the size of a bathtub. When we found it, it was filled with rainwater from a deep-throated thunderstorm which had washed over the mountain the day before. And in that rainwater—already in that short span of time—were hundreds of tadpoles. Gifts of thunder. It was such a wonderful thing to see, there on that otherwise dry mountain. We wanted to share it that dawn, to show our young writing students how quickly life can find ways to continue. But when we reached that indentation, there was no water. The dry air had sucked up that little pool. I looked at the dry stone, thinking for a moment that I might see the small dried bodies of tadpoles. But I saw nothing.

Then one of the students, Etheleen Poolaw, a young Kiowa Apache woman who had struggled to come up that dark mountainside, spoke. "Look!" she said, "look at them all." We looked to where she pointed and we saw them there, not just there, but all around us. All around us, like tiny dark stones come to life, were hundreds of small frogs, metamorphosed so quickly that some of them still had the remnants of tails. Now, as the sun rose and the mountaintop grew warmer, those small frogs were heading downslope, toward the more moist, shadier places below. Continuing the cycle of their ancestors. We all watched them for a long time and then, careful where we stepped, we, too, went down the mountain.

Such moments, moments free of denial and cynicism, have helped me continue to hear my Grandfather's voice and the voices of the others, old women and men, who walked the circle of this land long before people imported ideas of buying and selling Earth, as if it were an animal to be skinned and sold and then its useless remains discarded. It was just such a moment which came to me as I sat in that plane, somewhere over central New York, the long lines of the Finger Lakes below us. It came to me as a vision of the White Dog. It was clear and real—more real, in fact, than the memory I now hold of the seat I was in and the human voices around me. For though I felt no fear as I flew in that plane, I was feeling sorrow. It was a sorrow which I know grows more common every day to those of us who have been taught or been given through blood that hard gift of never forgetting that our bodies and spirits and the bodies and spirits of all living things about us are connected. The thought of what was happening to life on this earth had filled me with sadness. And then, in the place of despair, that moment came to me. I listened and sat for a time without moving. Then I said *"Niaweh!"* "Thank you." And I wrote in my journal these words—not as a completed poem, but as part of the journey:

The White Dog

After a day spent in Chicago
where a woman spoke to me
as if in a dream,
of how the animals all are dying,
I find myself inside an airplane.

I do not know how I have come
so far or at what cost
of oil surged out of wounded tundra
of smoke blackening lungs of sky
of metals heavier than breath
slowing the blood of living waters
so that I might join this rough passage,
stiff wings through razored air.

Yet, closing my eyes,
I hear Thunder's drum.
I am in a small room at Onondaga.
Just behind that curtain
carved basswood faces
of the Grandfathers hold
their patient knowing,
that circle which was
tomorrow yesterday.

In front of me I see the one
who has brought me here,
the White Dog, last of his people,
one of those animal messengers
who carry with their breaths
the prayer-filled smoke
up to Rawenio's Sky Land.

Its eyes are bright
as crystals, reflecting my face,
its stiff taxidermied limbs
hold the stance of a guardian.
It says, *Grandchild, there are ancient eyes*
measuring the people, waiting
your decisions,
choose as did the Good Mind,
to help life continue on earth.

Even from this diminished spring
the waters can deepen, again
be sweet for seven
generations
to come.

▲▼▲

It is sometimes hard to explain to people just what it is that you see
when you look at these worlds with something like a Native eye. Even

the words you speak may seem simple and clear but have another meaning. When you say "drum," do you see something to be played in a band or something, *some thing* to be made by an elementary school student in a crafts class in a "Native American Unit"? Or do you see a living creation, and does the word "drum," in whatever language it is spoken, mean to you the heartbeat of Earth? When you say the word "dog," is it a word which just means an animal or a word which is an insult? Or does it refer to one of the animal people, an honorable being, even a relative? The animals, you see, are seen as ancestors. When Native people speak of the time when animals could talk, they are speaking in the present tense.

How vastly different are the views of European and Native American insofar as our animal brothers and sisters are perceived when we talk about "hunting and fishing for sport." I was in Chicago to speak on Native American publishing at the American Library Association meeting. At that meeting on the panel with me was Paul DeMain, an enrolled member of the Oneida Nation, the editor of the Wisconsin Native newspaper *News from Indian Country*. There's been much written recently about the opposition (violent, at times) of white sports fishing groups to the Native people spearing fish, an exercise of their treaty rights (given to them in exchange for giving up the entire northern half of the state). Paul spoke of the importance of people understanding that there are different ways to see the same thing. "In our traditions," he said, "it's sacrilegious to pull a fish from the water, tear its mouth with a hook, damage the layer of protective slime on its body by taking it in your hand and then throw it back in. To us, that is not sport. If we hunted or fished, we had good reason to do so and we did it to provide for our people. But five hundred years ago, sport in Europe was the king's army chasing a fox through the forests, while our people here on this continent were playing lacrosse and ball games which were the ancestors of football and hockey, basketball, baseball and soccer."

The simple truth is, as Paul DeMain said, that sport to Europeans often meant the killing of nonhuman beings which wanted no part in that sport and were given no choice, while team sports, groups of men and women playing together in agreed-upon competition, was characteristic of the Native people of the Americas. That new idea of team sports, like the basic principles of democracy which the Founding Fathers borrowed from the Iroquois League, has been so wholeheartedly absorbed by white culture that there is hardly any awareness of its Native American roots. It is hard to communicate with people when they do not understand your language, though they think it is their own. And to really appreciate the writings of contemporary Native people, it is also necessary to have some understanding of the living cultures which shape their thoughts and language—which is why Paul DeMain spoke of sports and fishing as part of a discussion of Native publishing.

▲▼▲

We are now in the seventh generation of Native people since the coming of the Europeans five centuries ago. That period of five centuries, hard as it has been for Native people, is not seen by Indians as a long time. It is still commonly said by the Iroquois and other Native people that we must make our decisions, not just with tomorrow's result in mind, but thinking of how it will affect seven generations to come.

In one of the stories of the time of Creation, there were twin brothers. One was good-minded and cared for life on Earth. The other was hard-hearted, like flint. The Good Mind and Flint fought each other and when the Good Mind won, the hard-hearted brother was cast out—but not out of the minds of human beings. All of us have within us those two sides. We must recognize this, in order to choose the side of the Good Mind, to give good thoughts strength. So, as I speak of walking between the worlds, there is also that balance to keep in mind, that balance between the human power to destroy and the human ability to preserve.

It is a difficult time to be a storyteller and a writer—to see a world in such incredible turmoil, to recognize how much is threatened. In some cases, it turns the eyes of writers toward the decadent, toward the strange, perverse details of sex and violence to which they can connect for a momentary emotional jump start. It is not surprising, given the devalued currency of contemporary faith and the confusion between emotional riches and material wealth which seem to be common to much of mainstream America. It is also not surprising that the other side of that coin finds some Americans looking toward the Native people to find solutions. But here, too, there is often a lack of understanding. Native Americans are seen as symbols, as this decade's equivalent of the Maharishi or

Bagwan Rajneesh. Like Columbus, certain Americans get their Indians mixed up.

Trying to fill the emptiness in your heart, the hole in the American soul, with Indians, especially Indians seen as "mystic warriors," or "noble savages," no more real than the image on the old buffalo nickel, is both an exercise in self-deception and yet another form of racism. Understanding Native Americans does not mean becoming Indian. Understanding Native Americans begins with non-Indians understanding themselves. It is my belief—or at least my hope—that all human beings have that ability to walk between the worlds in their own ways. People who have worked hard on the kind of courageous self-awareness which characterize Alcoholics Anonymous programs do not become cynical or discouraged, but find within themselves spiritual depths they had not known existed—or had deliberately avoided acknowledging. In acknowledging a Higher Power, they are ready to acknowledge the workings of something greater than themselves in the world and the people around them.

It was dark when the plane landed in Albany and I walked toward my car in the lot. I looked, I am sure, no different from many others leaving that same airport. Few would notice the bear claw I wear around my neck or see the sweetgrass braid on the car's dashboard. Perhaps no one else leaving that airport would speak a few words of thanks and greeting to the wide Mohawk River as they crossed over it. But, though I share the words of my stories and poems—and this essay—with anyone who has the patience to read them, I do not carry that bear claw and that sweetgrass just so others can see them and, though I have much to be thankful for, I usually say my prayers of thanksgiving quietly. Indeed, as I started the engine and turned the wheel toward the north and the house where my Grandfather raised me, I knew that many things which others did not see were carrying me, helping me to stay in balance, guiding me like my Grandfather's voice. As I followed the light cast by my own passage along the dark road, I gave thanks for the gift of yet another day of walking between the worlds. Grandfathers, I thank you.

Ndakinna Means "Our Land"

Ndakinna means "Our Land." That is one of the words for home-ground among the Western Abenaki people who are my ancestors on my mother's side of the family. (As I have mentioned earlier, another half of my heritage is Slovak, a grandmother and grandfather who found themselves forced to leave their homeland forever to seek a new, freer land. But that story of the loss of home and the finding of new identities is one to tell in another book. My Slovak grandmother, Pauline Hrdlika Bruchac, once said to me: "We Slovaks were the Indians of Europe.")

That concept of home-ground, of the land being home in the widest sense of the word, is one of the things I love about that Indian part of my heritage. It is a sense of the earth itself, the whole land, not just the confines between walls and roof. It has shaped my way of seeing and walking. I know that, because of the lessons of my heritage, I can never view my home in as limited a way as do many of my non-Native friends. It has also led to my living, today, in the same house where I was raised by my grandparents. And that house, in the Adirondack foothills town of Greenfield Center, was built on the foundation of an older house owned by my great-grandparents before it was burned.

When you ask a Native American person about himself or herself, they will often begin by talking about their family. That is because our families make us who we are. I want to go one step further than that. To talk about myself, about my concept of home-ground, I must talk about that land which shaped my ancestors, that land which made us and continues to make us.

There is an old, old story told by the Abenaki people. In that story the Creator has finished making the earth. The dust of creation remains on the Creator's hands. The Creator, *Ktsi Nwaksw,* the "Great Mystery," brushes off that dust. It falls to the earth and the earth begins to shape itself. It shapes itself into a body and arms and hands and a head. Then that dust, that earth which shaped itself, sits up.

"Awani kia," says the Creator. "Who are you?"

"Odzihozo nia," that one answers. "I Am the One Who Shaped Himself."

Then Odzihozo began to drag himself about on the land, for he had not yet shaped legs. With his body he created mountains and lakes and the beds of rivers. The earth around us, here, in New England, made that first one and was shaped by that first one.

In the late 1980s I told that story in a courtroom in Vermont. I told it on behalf of the Abenaki Nation, for the trial was a trial focusing on fishing rights. To assert their ancient aboriginal rights, a large number of Abenaki people had deliberately fished without licenses and then insisted upon being tried in a court of law. The Abenaki are an unrecognized Native American tribal nation in the United States. We are here and we have been here and we have not gone away, yet for a century we have been an almost invisible presence. Until recently, the official histories of Vermont said that "there never were any Indians living in Vermont." If we lived there now, it wasn't really our home. Either that or we weren't really Indians.

In fact, Indians had learned early on to keep a low profile if they wished to go on living in Vermont. It became so dangerous in the 1800s to be an Indian in northern New England that the Western Abenaki people began to hide, as we put it, "in plain sight." We dressed and acted much like those around us, but there were always those of us who kept our stories, our traditions, our language and our understanding that this land is our home. My telling of that story was an assertion of our long relationship to the land, a relationship which goes back to the time when our land was shaped by the glaciers. I told other stories that day, stories which talk about *Ndakinna*.

My testimony was only a small part of the evidence which was offered, evidence given by people who had never forgotten their ties to a land which had sustained their ancestors and shaped their own lives to this day. The result of that trial was a victory for the Abenaki people. Clearly, the court decided, the Abenakis of Vermont were who they said they were. Native people still living in our own land. Two years later that decision would be overturned by the Vermont State Supreme Court, saying the "weight of history" made our claims no longer legal. Yet their history was a history of less than two centuries. Ours goes back ten thousand years. What seems old to modern-day Americans is newer than yesterday to those who live with a long memory of the land. Memories of home are the last memories to be forgotten.

There has been a long misunderstanding between the Native peoples of this land and those who came later, especially those who came from Europe, where land had become property, where "land speculation" and "land development" would effectively replace older European ideas of land as mother, land as sustainer, land as sacred. That view of land has produced an American culture which is both rootless and ruthless in relation to the earth. The idea of the frontier, of always moving on to a newer and better place, produced a culture of waste. Gold mining, which physically destroys the land (and is currently poisoning and tearing the lungs out of the Amazon rain forest of South America), is the most extreme example. That search for gold produced such by-products as the dispossession of the Cherokee Nation and the wholesale killing of the Indians of California by the Forty-Niners. The early pioneer heroes of that culture, people such as Daniel Boone, were, in fact, real estate speculators. When you look at the American landscape as a mother, as a home to be cherished, as do Native people, then the history of the "settlement of America" is an unmitigated tragedy.

To Native people, the land, this home-ground which sustains us, is alive. More than once, Native people answered Europeans seeking to buy their land with words like these spoken by Hinmaton Yalatkit ("Rolling Thunder in the Mountains"), the man best known to history as Chief Joseph: "The Earth and myself are of one mind." Then they would ask, "How can I sell my Mother?"

This vision of the wider earth as home was based not only in philosophy and in traditional stories, but also in the lifestyles of many Native peoples. Instead of having a village where one lived twelve months of the year, as would the new settlers of New England, there was a seasonal pattern of movement and migration. The winter village might be in one place, dependent upon food sources. The summer village would be in another. Several different sites might be used throughout the year, with no one place being the only permanent home, but all of those places being home-ground. Even the hunting territories were used in a cyclical fashion. No more than one-quarter of the hunting territory would be hunted in any one season so that the animals would not be wiped out. In the following year, a different quarter of that territory would be hunted. This led some to describe Native people as nomadic, with the implication that they were "people of no fixed abode," and "homeless wanderers." The truth is that ours was a circle of habitation, a home in many places.

The Abenaki were no exception. Each family tended to be associated with a watershed, moving up or down it, from riverbank to highlands and back again in a seasonal flow. Communities were relatively small, often no more than half a dozen wigwoms, dome-shaped or cone-shaped structures made of saplings covered with a blanket of birch bark shingles. In Abenaki *maska* is "blanket," *maskwa* is "birch bark," *maskwamozi* is the "birch bark tree." Our homes were given to us by the trees which would take off their blankets to give us shelter. Our language reminded us that our homes were an organic part of the world around us.

Each wigwom was the dwelling of no more than one or two families. In the spring season, those wigwoms would be near such good fishing spots as the lower falls on the Winooski River in Vermont by the "salmon hole," a place still known to fishermen today. Then crops would be planted on the good alluvial soils. In the spring and summer, the ripening berries would draw parties of pickers to the places where the strawberry ripened, followed by the raspberry, the blueberry and the blackberry, returning home in early fall for the harvest of the corn. In the autumn and winter, people would move upland to the villages which were hunting camps, following the moose and the deer and the caribou on snowshoes. Traditional names still found in the Native languages of the Northeast for the different moons of the year reflect that pattern of wide habitation. September is *Skamonkas,* the "Corn Moon," while March is *Mozokas,* the "Moose Moon."

Among our neighbors to the west, the Haudenosaunee or "People of the Longhouse," those called Iroquois today, things were a little different. By the twelfth century, the Iroquois people were living in large seemingly permanent villages, often with dozens of longhouses, each of which could hold as many as a hundred people (or more). These Native towns were supported by huge fields planted with the Three Sisters—Corn, Beans and Squash—and by the hunting of the deer, for clothing as well as for food. Their villages did not have a seasonal pattern of movement. (Along the eastern shores of Lake Champlain, where my Abenaki ancestors grew large fields of corn like those of the Iroquois, Abenaki wigwoms were often replaced by longhouses, and villages assumed a more permanent character.)

However, among the Haudenosaunee, there would come a time, perhaps after a period of ten or twelve years, when the fields were tired, when the great longhouses covered with bark would begin to decay, when the deer would become scarce. Then it would be time to move the village. All of the people would leave that old village site and move to a new place, some miles away. It was called moving the village because the name of the village moved with the people. Eventually, decades later, when all traces of the old village were gone and the land had fully recovered, that same site would be occupied again. However far you traveled, you would always eventually return. If not yourself, then your children's children. Again, there was a circle of habitation, a wide view of home.

There are two stories of homecoming that I want to share. The first is my own. After being raised in that house in Greenfield Center by my maternal grandparents I went off to college. My grandmother had died when I was sixteen, but my grandfather, Jesse Bowman, remained there. He was waiting for me to return. He continued to run the little general store and gas station, which he had built next to the old house. He seldom made any money, for he trusted everyone and allowed them to write what they owed him in his account book. I think that trust, like his philosophy of gentle child rearing which had been given him by his own parents, was one of the legacies of his Abenaki ancestry. In the old days, among our people, a man was only as good as his word. If you promised to do something, you would do it. It didn't matter if there were no witnesses and no written papers. The land could hear you, and the land would remember. And my grandfather always looked at the land with respect.

I think my grandfather made such a promise to the land. He would wait there for me, keep our home until I could return home. When I married and then went on to graduate school he was still waiting, now keeping that home-ground for me and my new wife, Carol. When Carol and I volunteered to teach in West Africa for three years and then had our first son, Jim, my grandfather still held on to that promise he had made to himself and to the land. He kept our home for us to come back to.

Those were hard times in America. It was the end of the 1960s, a time of rebellion and uncertainty, the assassination of leaders, the start of a loss of innocence, the hard time of the Vietnam War. I was not sure we would ever return to the United States when we left for Ghana in

1966. Yet my grandfather's faith and the love of the land did call me back home. In the fall of 1969 we returned to Greenfield Center, moved into the old house and stayed. Late that winter, my grandfather passed on. Our family doctor told me that my grandfather had so many things wrong with him, from lung cancer to pernicious anemia, that it was a wonder he had managed to hang on as long as he did.

"He could have died four years ago," Doc Magovern said, "but he was bound and determined to see you come home."

And so he did. Though his body has gone back to the dust of our land, his spirit is alive. And his presence is always here with me in the house that has been our family home for five generations, in the gardens he planted that I now plant, in the stream where he helped me catch my first fish, in the paths through the woods we first walked together picking berries when I was barely able to stand on my own. He still reminds me that this place is my home, that caring for it is my responsibility, that we will always be part of the land.

The second story is one that I thought I would not live to tell, for it is a story of another larger return, a homecoming that was prophesied two hundred years ago. After the American Revolution, the Mohawk people were dispossessed of their homeland in the Mohawk Valley of New York State. They found themselves forced to move north. Two of their communities found themselves on small tracts of land along the St. Lawrence River—the St. Regis Reservation which is half in Canada and partly in the United States and Kahnawake, the "Rapids Place," a village name which had once been given to lands along the Mohawk River in New York State.

To the west of the city of Amsterdam, there along the Mohawk River, there is an ancient village site. Archaeologists have found, there, the remains of not one or two but many different villages from long ago, each one built on top of the remains of an older one which was left behind in that ancient pattern of moving the village. That site has been known as Kanatsiohareke, the "Place of the Clean Pot." The nearby village of Canajoharie is simply a misspelling of that Mohawk name. On that village site of Kanatsiohareke the county ran a farm for the impoverished elderly.

There was a prophecy spoken in the early days of the Mohawk removal. One day we will return to our homeland. It seemed a distant dream. Edmund Wilson's nonfiction book *Apologies to the Iroquois* was published in 1960. Part of that book tells how one Mohawk visionary, a man named Standing Arrow, tried to make that prophecy come true in the late 1950s, camping with a small band of followers on land along Schoharie Creek. Eventually their occupation failed, though similar attempts at reclaiming Indian homeland would continue to take place in New York and other parts of the country over the next three decades— from Alcatraz Island in San Francisco Bay to Yellow Thunder Camp in the Black Hills of South Dakota. Such attempts are still taking place. There is a very long memory of home in the hearts of the Native peoples of North America.

In the last few years, another group of Mohawk people, led by Tom Porter, a nephew of that same Standing Arrow, began to raise money to purchase land in the Mohawk Valley. Their aim was to start a community which would honor their old homeland, a place where the Mohawk language would be spoken, a place free of gambling and violence, of drugs and alcoholism. It seemed like a dream until an unexpected donation was given to them, and their bid was accepted at an auction which sold off that five hundred acres which had once been a county farm. In 1994 Kanatsiohareke was born again. The village had come home. There, along the Mohawk River, a kind of healing had begun.

▲▼▲

When we are at home in the natural world, we are whole. We are whole not just physically, but also in mind and in spirit. It is a wholeness which preserves and sustains. It is neither romantic nor otherworldly. It is deeply, urgently practical.

The ecological sense of the Native view of land as home is evident. Native people understood that we must treat our homes with respect. Just as a modern person, today, would not be likely to set fire to his or her own carpet or break one's own windows, so, too, in the old days would it be regarded as strange for a person to seek to kill all the game animals, to cut down all the trees, to make the water so dirty that the fish would die and the water would be unfit to drink. One might move, but one did not move on. It was understood that no matter where we went during our lives, we did not leave the earth behind. It is an understanding that is desperately needed today if we wish, as Americans, as human beings, to find our way back home again. It is an understanding not only for this generation, but for the generations to come.

MIZI NEWETKAMIGWEZO
"THE FAMILIES GATHERED TOGETHER"

✵

There has been, since the coming of the first Europeans to the Americas, a history of trying to "settle" the Native peoples. Despite the evidence of such long-established indigenous city civilizations as those of the Inca, the Aztec and the Maya, the picture most often painted of pre-Columbian Native Americans is that of nomadic peoples with no real homes. The idea of the city was seen as a foreign concept to the Indian, and "civilizing" or even urbanizing the Indians for their own good would be used as a justification for centuries of policies which worked toward the eradication of already existing Native cultures.

The destruction of the Native peoples of the Caribbean at the hands of the Spanish was done—or at least its doing was justified—in the interest of creating "ordered communities" to save souls. The *encomienda,* a system which gave Spaniards control of the lives of the Taino peoples of such islands as Cuba, Puerto Rico and Hispaniola, was justified to the church and the Spanish crown as a necessity in order to turn uncivilized heathens into Christians. The *encomienda* system, it was said, would settle these people who were mere "wanderers," people with no fixed abode into communities for the first time. There, cared for by their Spanish lords, they would be given the blessings of the true faith. In actuality, of course, what they were given were brief lives of harsh slavery where such new European diseases as smallpox and influenza could quickly run their course among people weakened by hunger and overwork. Within fifty years, the original native population of the Caribbean—perhaps as many as a million souls—was reduced to a few thousand.

The double irony of the *encomienda* story and of other attempts—from the disastrous reservation systems to the more recent relocation programs after World War II which took people from the reservations and placed them in large cities, effectively creating Native American ghettoes—made to "help" the supposedly rootless indigenous peoples of the continent by bringing them the benefits of European-style communities is that the indigenous peoples of the Americas were never "wanderers" with no real tradition of community. Universally, the many Native nations of North America have strongly developed traditions of people living together in ordered societies, in villages, towns and even cities, long before the European invasions.

Although, as among the Abenaki people of the Northeast in the period before European contact or horse nations of the Great Plains such as the Cheyenne and Lakota in the eighteenth and nineteenth centuries, the highly portable homes of Native peoples might be moved from one place to the other in the course of a round of seasons, there was nothing aimless or disordered about these regular movements of population. European Americans still persist in describing the Native people as nomadic or rootless but this was far from the truth. Instead, the indigenous Americans saw their home as a larger one, encompassing the familiar and familial natural world around them. They understood how to live together, often in societies in which there were no police, no jails and no need for either. And their stories and traditions resonate with that sense of the world as their city where the human people were regarded as a part of a large, well-ordered community seen in terms of an extended family.

If there was antipathy between the Indian and the city, it was between the indigenous concept of communities, however large, as being extended families versus the European city made up of people who were largely strangers to each other. When, in 1886, Black Elk accompanied the Buffalo Bill Wild West Show, he was so struck by the way the *Wasichus* treated each other in their cities that he made the following comment in *Black Elk Speaks:*

> After a while I got used to being there, but I was like a man who had never had a vision. I felt dead and my people seemed lost and I thought I might never find them again. I did not see anything to help my people. I could see that the *wasichus* did not care for each other the way my people did before the nation's hoop was broken. They would take everything from each other if they could, and so there were some who had more of everything than they could use, while crowds of people had nothing at all and maybe were starving. They had forgotten that the earth was their mother.[1]

That sense of the dislocation and the loss of balance in the modern city remains a common perception on the part of Native Americans. My Pueblo/Apache friend Swift Eagle told me about his first visit to Los Angeles and Hollywood in the 1930s. He stood on a street corner shaking his head for a long time. Finally a policemen came up to him.

"What are you looking for?" the policeman said.

"I am looking for civilization," Swift Eagle answered. "Do you have any of that here?"

▲▼▲

One generalization which may be made about the layout and structure of the buildings found in Native towns, villages and cities, a generalization that holds true throughout much of the continent and is echoed in traditional stories, is that Native houses were directed toward rather than away from nature. Native homes were invested with deeply symbolic meanings. For example, whether plain's tipis, southwest pueblos or northeastern longhouses, buildings were usually constructed with their doorways to the east, where the sun rose each day. The architecture of Native buildings reflected an awareness of and a direct relation to the natural world. The roof stands for the sky. The sides correspond to the four directions, the floor is the earth. In *Respect for Life,* a series of discussions with Native elders that took place in 1974, Henry Old Coyote, a Crow elder, talked about the intricate symbolism of each part of the tipi lodge. The first tipi was given to a Crow hero by none other than Old Man, the Sun, to honor him for slaying monsters that threatened the people. "The tipi itself represents a woman," Old Coyote said, "... it represents the woman and that every day as you face a new day you are born all over again." Leaving the lodge each morning was thus a symbolic act, like the birth of a child to its first dawn. Victor Sarracino, a Laguna elder, then spoke of Pueblo traditions of house building, showing a similar awareness of that deep interrelation of all things. As with the tipi, Sarracino said, "Pueblos usually have their doorways facing east so that the inhabitants can greet the rising sun each day and ask for blessings for the new day." Moreover, Sarracino said, the very act of building a home had to be undertaken with great care because "the Laguna tribe has always understood this earth to be its mother."[2]

Among the Native peoples of the Americas, therefore, community is not separate from nature. The idea of a city being an "un-natural" place is a foreign concept. The nature of the natural world permeates human communities. All cities feel nature, but the European city has most often tried to ignore it, fight against it or miniaturize it into the manageable form of the city park or garden. The Native view is radically different. In fact, through Native eyes, the natural world is seen to include humans and exists in terms of communities—not just communities of human people, but also communities of animal people, plant people and so on. Not only is everything seen as alive, everything is also sentient and ordered. As Christine Mitchell, an Akwesasne Mohawk elder, explained it to me, when one goes into the forest to pick plants for medicine, one looks not for an isolated plant, but for a community of plants. Then one does not pick the biggest plant. That plant is regarded as the leader of that little community, the chief or the mother of the others. Instead, after stating one's intention to that community of plants, one should pick a smaller plant, one which may sacrifice itself without harming the integrity of that community. Further, the person gathering the plants must place something in exchange for that plant—perhaps an offering of tobacco. Then, if there are seeds on the plant which has been picked, one must loosen the earth and plant those seeds.

One of the stories told among a number of the Native nations of the area now called New England and eastern Canada is that of the Deer Wife. A hunter goes into the forest and encounters a beautiful, graceful woman who offers to marry him. He goes with her to the village of her people. Though he does not realize it at first, these people are all deer. The understanding of who these fine-looking people—who appear to be human beings—really are only comes to him when he says he is hungry.

"Come with me," says one of the young men. "I will turn into a deer and you may shoot me and eat me. But when you have eaten me, you must go down to the river and place all of my bones into the water."

The young man does as he is told and when he arrives back at the village from the river, he finds the young man there waiting for him. So he understands that the deer which the people hunt only give up their bodies and survive in spirit, as long as the people treat them respectfully and hunt in the proper way.

▲▼▲

In what is now known as New England, the area the Abenaki people refer to as *Ndakinna,* "Our Land," a tradition existed of gathering the people together at certain times. Though, in some areas for much of the year, people might live in relatively small villages of a few related families, there were also larger communities which might number in the thousands. However, as large as those communities might have been, the importance of relationship and balance was not forgotten. If we look at the Abenaki language of clues as to how people saw themselves and their communities, we find that the word for tribe in Abenaki is *negewetkamigwezo,* literally "those of one family." The term for nation is *mizi negewetkamigwezo,* which means the "families gathered together."

It is sometimes suggested that Native nations only enjoyed ecological and social stability because there were so few people. If there were more Indians, it is said, then they would have lost that balance. My own belief is to the contrary. The maintenance of that balance meant that Native communities in pre-Columbian America not only could grow to impressively large sizes, but they could vanish also without leaving the sorts of scars on their environment to mark their passing which are left by modern communities. That vanishing might be due to the ravages of European diseases or it might be due to the nature of community in Abenaki eyes. Because the primary building block of an Abenaki Nation was the family, then events such as war or famine could mean that the families gathered together would disperse. Instead of being an unwieldy giant locked in one place, a city was a living organism which could change its shape and location and survive. Among the neighboring Iroquois, a village would be occupied for a period of years until the soil grew infertile, then the buildings would be abandoned and the village would move. Its people and the name of the village, both, would relocate. One contemporary example is the current Mohawk village of Caughnawaga, or Kahnawake, located across the river from Montreal. Originally, Caughnawaga was in the Mohawk valley more than two hundred miles to the south.

How big were some of those Native cities of the Northeast, those gatherings of families? In 1993 and 1994, my son Jesse did extensive research in the *Jesuit Relations,* letters written by the early French Jesuit priests to relate their activities in the New World. In the Relation of 1657–1658, which includes letters written by Paul Regueneau and

Garbriel Druillettes, the following information can be found in a summary of the Abenaki communities found within a week's journey of the village of St. Michel near the St. Lawrence River. After listing villages of varying sizes, each succeeding village larger than the one before, the Relation states:

> La cinquieme Nation, qui fe nomme de Aliniouek, eft plus nombreaufe: on y compte bien 20000. hommes, & foixante Bourgs: ce font enuiron cent mille ames. Elle eft a fept iournees de S. Michel, vers l'Ouest.[3]

Think of that, "twenty thousand men and sixty villages" and "a hundred thousand souls in all." Although Aliniouek exists in that Relation, which records the names of many now-vanished communities, there was no physical evidence to mark its place on the map. Gone like a fish through the water, leaving not even a ripple behind. Yet the blueprint of that Native city, a city not at war with the natural world, remains in Native traditions and in Native hearts. It lives wherever our families are gathered together.

Notes

1. J. G. Neihardt, *Black Elk Speaks* (New York: Simon & Schuster, 1932).
2. Sylvester M. Morey and Olivia L. Gilliam, eds., *Respect for Life: The Traditional Upbringing of American Indian Children* (New York: Myrin Institute, 1980).
3. Reuben Gold Thwaites, ed. *The Jesuit Relations and Allied Documents: Travels and Explorations of the Jesuit Missionaries in New France, 1610–1791* (Cleveland: The Burrows Brothers Co., 1896–1901).

As Equal as Earth Is to Sky

The Balanced Roles of
Native American Men and Women

There is a saying in European culture—"What you see is what you get." Take that saying slightly out of context and apply it to the way the majority culture has seen the roles and relationships of men and women in the Native cultures of North America and what we get is a picture of men and women as distorted as the image seen in a fun-house mirror. There has always been a problem of vision—or the lack of it—when it comes to the way European cultures have seen the first inhabitants of this hemisphere. Because they were from societies where the roles of women had been limited for centuries, where uncounted numbers of wise women and herbalists had been classified as witches and murdered, where a man was regarded in the nearsighted eyes of the law as the owner of his wife (even as he might own a horse or a dog), those first European explorers and settlers framed (or, better yet, put blinders on) their visions of Native life and Native people in ways which created images of "wild Indians," which I, as a person of Native ancestry, find incredibly inaccurate and demeaning and yet, sadly, these images still remain the norm.

What was it that they saw? And even more importantly, what is the truer picture of Native lives and gender relationships which they totally missed or badly misinterpreted? Let me, from the perspective of a person of mixed Native and European ancestry, tell you what I have learned to see of both sides as I have grown up looking back and forth between those two worlds. My perspective is that of one who has been blessed with some of the best things which both worlds have to offer, giving me an education on one side which is strongly based in the academic world and, on the other side, in the tradition of listening long and carefully to the elders while also paying close attention to the natural world which surrounds us with its own lessons.

We have only to look at our everyday language used in relation (often unconsciously) to Native people to pick up the prejudices and distortions which have become part of the majority culture's view of Native women and men. Some of that language has its origin in fact, but fact which has been so misunderstood as to make fact into fiction or, worse yet, demeaning stereotype. How about the parents who tell their children to stop acting like "wild Indians"? How about the game we all grew up with called "cowboys and Indians"? How about all the high school, college and professional sports' teams named after Indians, prompting every newspaper in America at least once or twice each year to run headlines in their sports pages which summarize the results of a football game something along the line of "Indians Scalp Pioneers in 40-0 Massacre"?

Or take the term "Indian giver," used to describe someone who gives a gift and then demands it back. Behind that term is an image of Native people as insincere, even treacherous, lacking in true generosity. Its origins probably come from certain little known aspects of Native culture. For example, certain gifts were meant to be shared, to "keep moving." A material object might be given to someone with the understanding that they would use it and then, when finished with it, they would either return it or give it to someone else.

The kind of strict possessiveness, which characterized European cultures at the time of first contact with Native cultures in the Western Hemisphere in the fifteenth and sixteenth centuries, was foreign to the Native people of the Northeast. Personal possessions tended to be relatively few and if someone had a special object—often something which related to that person's spiritual life, such as a pipe or a medicine bundle, or even just a personal stone knife which would be constantly in use in everyday work—that object would be carried on the person's body (knives were often hung about one's neck from a thong) and kept out of sight when not in use, for example, in a box under a person's bed. Things which were left out in plain sight were regarded by many Native cultures as free for anyone to take and use. That sort of European possessiveness (once it is mine, it is mine alone, and I will even kill to keep it!) extended into ideas of ownership which were so profoundly different from the ideas of Native people that many Native people find them hard to understand to this day. I have already mentioned the European idea of a man owning his wife. (Until this century, though it might not be approved of by his community, a white man could beat his wife and children—even to the point of death—without fear of *legal* consequences. If such attitudes seem strange to you, then let me point out that they still exist in many places—including countless police departments which refuse to intervene on the part of battered wives.)

Linked to that is the strange—to a Native mind—concept of owning the land and selling it as one might barter the skin of an animal. Though different groups of Native people, a tribal nation, for example, might claim "ownership" of areas of land and might even engage in conflict with another tribal nation over control of a hunting ground, such ownership was more in the realm of stewardship or caretaking. Individual ownership and the practice of accumulating great plots of land in the hands of a single person who uses it only for personal enrichment is regarded as profoundly unbalanced and antisocial behavior. Earth, Native people appear to universally believe (throughout the entire Western Hemisphere), is female, is nurturing, is alive, is our Mother. Earth, like a human mother, is the source of birth and the sustaining of life.

It has been said directly to me countless times by Native elders—Abenaki and Iroquois from the Northeast; Cherokee, Chickahominy and Seminole from the South; Cheyenne and Lakota from the West; Colville and Nez Perce from the Northwest; Pueblo and Navajo from the Southwest; Mayan from Mexico; Inupiaq and Athabascan from Alaska—that we must care for the earth, not just for ourselves, but for the generations to come. That nurturing and, in Western eyes, feminine attitude is characteristic of both women and men. "We must always think of how the things we do will affect seven generations to come," said Oren Lyons, a man who is one of the Faithkeepers of the Onondaga Nation of the Iroquois, when we were doing a storytelling program together at the Onondaga Indian School several years ago. (A 1991 PBS special in which Oren Lyons was interviewed by Bill Moyers is one television program that I strongly recommend.)

With such dramatically different views, it is no wonder that what Europeans "got" when they thought they were "seeing" Native cultures was in fact only a reflection of their own preconceptions. Rather than looking, open-eyed, through a window, they were squinting into a mirror. Let us focus our gaze now on some of those images of the roles of men and women given us by those early European observers of Native cultures in New England.

"The men employ their time wholly in hunting and in other exercises of the bow except that they sometimes take some pains at fishing. The women live a most slavish life: they carry all the burdens, set and dress their corn, gather it in and seek out for much of their food, beat and make ready the corn to eat and have all household care lying upon them."[1] So wrote Governor Edward Winslow of Plymouth in the early 1600s. In that same period an Englishman named Christopher Levette observed that "their wives are their slaves and doe all their work: The men doe nothing but kill Beasts, Fish etc."[2] There are countless such observations from that period, not only in New England, but throughout the range of the coast where the first European colonies had gained tentative footholds. The lot of the Indian "squaw" was drudgery. (The word "squaw" comes from Algonquin and is a suffix applied to indicate feminine gender or to refer to female genitals. It is a word which has become loaded with pejorative meaning and is regarded as an insult by virtually all contemporary Native women. Yet the word continues to be used by some people. It is yet another example of the way our everyday language about Native people creates and preserves stereotypes.) Meanwhile, those early chroniclers concluded, as his wife slaved, the Indian "brave" lived an easy, even lazy existence. Two centuries later, in the 1800s, George Catlin, the famous painter of Indians, held much the same view, using the word "slaves" to describe Native women of the western tribal nations.[3]

What was it that these early (and later) white observers saw or did not see which led them to the conclusion that Indian women were disenfranchised drudges and slaves, Indian men lazy drones who did little but hunt and fish and make war? For one, the majority of those who have written about sexual roles and the relationship between Native men and women have been white males who have not been—as contemporary ethnologists put it—"participant observers." The roles of women have been so poorly understood and so denigrated in European culture for so many centuries that it is no wonder these male European observers, blind to what the real lives and the human potential of their own female counterparts were, did not perceive the Native women of the New World clearly. In all fairness, it should be said that not every white male observer in the 1600s saw things the same way. It is just that such voices as that of Roger Williams—who described the way Indian women formed circles to learn news and debate the business of their tribal nation—seem to have been lost in the forming of the public notion in the majority society (then and now) of how it was for Native women.[4]

Native cultures of this hemisphere, past and present, divided responsibilities between men and women in a way which was as equal as the partnership between Earth and Sky. Between the two of them, the work was accomplished which nurtured the social, religious and economic lives of their nations—just as the sun and rain which come from Father Sky combine with Mother Earth to bring forth crops each year. The concept of the Sky as a Father also seems to enjoy wide currency among the Native people of this hemisphere. Considering the importance of the sky for agriculture and the fact that Native peoples of this hemisphere were among the greatest agriculturalists of all time, it should not be surprising that this complementary male-female relationship between Earth and Sky is so common to hundreds of tribal nations and that the metaphor of Earth and Sky should be applied to relationships between human women and men.

The lives of many Native peoples—such as the Mohegan, the Wampanoag, the Pequot and the Abenaki, who are among the original peoples of the area which became known as New England—depended upon an economy based equally on food from the earth provided by the women (gathering berries and roots and herbs, cultivating plants such as corn, squash and beans grown in communally cared-for gardens) and foods from the forests, streams, lakes and sea obtained by the men through the rigorous and demanding pursuits of hunting and fishing. Thus it seems only logical that the roles of both women and men should have been held in equal esteem by Native cultures dependent upon both for their continuance. Physically, Native men and women were well matched. Both led vigorous lives, and Europeans in the first centuries of contact are nearly unanimous in remarking on the physical beauty, glowing health and strength (and size—the average Indian in the Northeast, the Great Lakes region and the Plains appears to have towered over the average European according to early European visitors who spoke of the great height of the Indians) of both women and men. Though men tended to be a bit larger and stronger than women, suiting them better for certain tasks of physical labor, the intellectual capacity and the spiritual capacity of men and women were generally regarded as equal. Moreover, if a woman was strong enough and interested enough in doing so, she could choose to play roles usually taken by men, going hunting and fishing, becoming a warrior, becoming a chief.

At this point a few words about the "warrior" tradition are in order. Among most Native people, being a warrior does not necessarily mean being a person who loves killing. A warrior is one who fights to defend the people. That is the case with virtually every famous "Indian Warrior" who tried to protect his people during the Indian wars of the last four centuries. Sitting Bull, Geronimo, Chief Joseph, Crazy Horse, Tecumseh, Pontiac, Dragging Canoe, King Phillip (Metacomet) and innumerable others were all great warriors, but they were also men who loved their families and their Native nations deeply. It was important for a man to show his bravery when he did have to fight in a war, but it was just as important for a war leader to bring his men home safely after a battle as it was to secure a great victory. In a surprising number of cases, in fact, war is regarded as a spiritually damaging experience, and men who had been to war and touched the enemy had to go through a long "Enemy Way" curing ceremony among the Navajo. The Hopi forbade all warfare, calling themselves the People of Peace. Among the Iroquois, a man could not be a chief if he had ever fought in a war and any chief who went to war lost his chieftaincy. War leaders were respected among the Iroquois, but they were not chiefs and could not make decisions on behalf of the nation. Such attitudes toward warfare may seem surprisingly "unmanly," yet they produced some of the greatest warriors in history.

In *Boys Will Be Boys: Breaking the Link between Masculinity and Violence,* the social philosopher Myriam Miedzian discusses ways in which team sports, as practiced by far too many coaches and parents, encourage cruelty and violent behavior—winning at any cost—in young men. She makes the point that such violence is then carried off the playing field in their relations with women and cites as one example the fact that about one-third of all campus assaults on women are by athletes. I find her point particularly telling when I consider the fact that the modern team sports of the world, quite literally, have their roots in Native cultures. When Europeans came to the Western Hemisphere in the fifteenth and sixteenth centuries, they came from cultures with only one real team sport—warfare! Nearly all European athletic competitions were based on the skills of war—archery, wrestling, javelin throwing, races on horseback or on foot and so on. The rubber ball did not exist in Europe. (I am aware that there are some other theories about the origins of team sports, such as soccer originating with the kicking of decapitated heads after one battle or another, but I am also aware of very firm evidence of the actual existence of team sports for many centuries in pre-Columbian America.) What the Europeans found in the New World were Native people in Mexico playing basketball with teams and a rubber ball in a sunken court with a stone hoop; Native people in the Northeast playing lacrosse; Native people in the South and Midwest playing hockey.

What they did not find, however, were the contemporary attitudes toward sports that we find now in coaches and parents and university athletic programs thirsting for play-off bucks and bowl bids. When lacrosse was played among the Native people of the Northeast, it was often in great games with one village against another. The two goals were in each village—sometimes miles apart—and everyone who could stand and hold up a lacrosse stick, women and men, old and young, would play. Further, lacrosse was a sacred game. The motion of the ball through the air symbolized the passage of the sun across the sky and it was said that even the sky beings such as the great Thunderbirds played lacrosse. The real goal of the game was more than one side beating the other, for such games were often played as a prayer, played in honor of a person who was ill in the belief that this game and its great energy would contribute toward making that person well again. When Handsome Lake, the Iroquois prophet, came to Onondaga in his final days, in August 1815, a lacrosse game was played in his honor in the hope it would heal him.

Also, team sports were not always segregated—with men playing men and women playing women as is the case today. One of the biggest battles we have seen in children's sports has been waged around girls wanting to play "boys" games such as football. Yet it was traditional among the Shawnee for the men to play yearly against the women in a rough and tumble ball game which was something like a combination of American football and soccer. Each side tried hard to win, for the losers would have to do such tasks as gathering firewood, but the game itself was also a part of a sacred round of traditional ceremonies with more meaning to it than just a sports contest. From what I have been told, those games were always very even. It seems that a different spirit of competition would be fostered by team sports played in this way than that spirit of insensitive aggression so rightly condemned by Miedzian.

Just as Native women could play roles commonly taken by men, the reverse was also true for their male counterparts. In a number of Native tribal nations, a man who was born with a woman's spirit (and saying this was not regarded as an insult—as it is, today, among American men who are told from boyhood not to be sissies or to act like girls) could choose to dress and act as a woman throughout his life. *Berdache,* a word referring to a man who dresses in women's clothing and combines the work and social roles of both sexes is the term used by the Lakota Sioux to refer to this third sex in a matter-of-fact way. In many tribal nations, such individuals are treated with great respect and honor. A friend of mine from the Crow Nation told me that among his people in the past such men-women were always regarded as the best teachers of the young. One famous southwestern *berdache,* whose name was We'wha and who was described as the strongest and tallest member of her Zuni Nation, was brought to Washington in 1886 by the anthropologist Matilda Stevenson. "Princess" We'wha mingled with the elite of Washington, demonstrated Zuni arts and crafts (We'wha was an extremely talented artist) and shook hands with President Grover Cleveland. All this took place without anyone in Washington society ever suspecting We'wha was not a woman.[5]

Further, because only women could accomplish the miracle of birth, their powers were seen as even greater than those of men in a number of Native cultures. Because of a woman's power to renew and cleanse her own body—through her monthly menstrual cycle—it was not as necessary for her to undergo such strenuous cleansing ceremonies as the sweat lodge. (However, the sweat lodge was also used by woman in many Native nations, though never when she was in her menses.) That power was so great that it could nullify male power, and so a woman in her cycle was supposed to seclude herself, often with other women also having their periods, in a lodge separate from the rest of the village. Until her cycle was completed she was able to meditate, to rest and to enjoy that time with her fellow women. Time with fellow women was of great importance. The social lives of the women were linked in numerous ways, including through special ceremonies, societies (such as the Society of Women Planters among the Iroquois) and communal work. When it came time to plant, weed or harvest, the women would go in communal work groups to one field after another. In such social groups, where singing and joking were always present, the work went fast and seemed more like play.

It should also be noted that women were the rulers of their own bodies. A woman could choose who she would or would not marry and even after marriage could refuse her husband's sexual advances. Numerous methods of birth control appear to have been used—particularly medicinal plants which prevented pregnancy. If a woman felt her husband was mean or unsuitable, she could leave him at any time or, in the case of the Iroquois, tell him to go home to his mother's lodge. The picture of the Indian woman as a poorly treated, overworked creature is totally untrue. May Jemison, a white woman who was taken captive by the Seneca in the eighteenth century, refused to return to white society and lived out her life as an Indian by choice. Her observation of Native women's lives was that "their task is probably not harder than white women, and their cares are certainly not half as numerous or so great."[6]

▲▼▲

Most of the Europeans who first observed the relationship between Native men and women did not understand what they were really seeing for many reasons. These white men came from a culture where hunting and fishing was a leisure time activity, a sport, not serious work. When they saw Native men "lying around, while their wives worked," those men were not lazy slackers, they were recuperating from the rigors of hunting and respecting the fact that the women did not wish to be interfered with in the work which they knew best. Because the wild animals were regarded as beings worthy of respect—as Animal People—being a hunter carried a heavy moral and spiritual responsibility. Hunting did not begin or end with killing an animal. Only certain animals could be taken—you could not kill a female animal with young, for example. And before hunting, one might have to observe certain rules, not eat certain things, perform certain ceremonies. In a similar way, after hunting, one was obligated to the spirit of the animal just killed to appease that animal's spirit in such a way that it would not prevent the hunter from having future success. The Cherokee writer, Marilou

Awiakta, tells the story of Awi Usdi, the little white deer who is the leader of the game animals. If a Cherokee hunter does something which is morally wrong in hunting—kills a female animal with young, for example—then Awi Usdi will come to that hunter in the night and inflict him with rheumatism so that he becomes crippled.[7] Many hunters were not allowed to eat the game they killed but had to hunt for the others of their village. Hunting was not, as in Europe, a sport in which one engaged purely for amusement. It was life itself.

When these same European men saw the Native women engaged in the tasks of farming and domestic work, once again they did not see what was really happening. They did not recognize, for example, that in many Native cultures it is the woman who is regarded as the head of the household and the owner of the house. Among the Iroquois, each of the great bark-shingled longhouses (which might hold as many as twenty or more families) belonged to a particular clan. Among the Mohawk Nation of the Iroquois those clans were Turtle, Bear and Wolf. Each clan was headed by a Clan Mother. No one could enter that longhouse without her permission. When a man married, he had to leave the longhouse of his mother and move to the longhouse of his wife's clan. (You were not supposed to marry someone from your own clan.) When children were born, they belonged to the clan of their mother—the equivalent socially of a child having the same last name as the father in European culture. Because of their preoccupation with the lives of the male "warriors," the majority of European observers of the Iroquois did not realize they were looking at a culture which was matrilocal, matrilineal and woman centered! Taking it one step further, the men who were the leaders of the Iroquois Nations, the men chosen to be Faithkeepers or "Chiefs" and represent their individual nations in the Grand Council meetings of the Five Nation Confederacy, were all chosen by the women of their clan. Only the women could raise a man up to be a chief. And if he did not behave properly, the women would warn him three times and then take him out of office! It was hard enough for Europeans accustomed to lifetime rule by kings and czars and a hereditary nobility to accept the fact that the Native peoples of the New World actually chose their own leaders and could remove them from office. But the idea that in some Native nations women were the ones who did the choosing? That was unthinkable!

Yet, if we examine the historical record, we find clear evidence that there were always a few of those European observers who actually saw the reality or, even if they didn't know what they were seeing, recorded enough of it for us to put it together and recognize it—just as in that Arabian parable of the blind men and the elephant where each person felt only one part of the animal and drew an incorrect conclusion about its appearance, putting all the parts together can give us the truer picture. It is recorded by some European chroniclers that a number of the tribal nations of New England had women leaders in the 1600s. When the chief of the Pocasset Nation died, it was Weatamoo, a woman, who was chosen as chief—not her husband, whose name was Petononowett. The Quinnipiacs (in the area now known as Guilford, Connecticut) were led by a woman sachem named Shaumpishuh.[8]

Just for comparison, let us consider the view of women's and men's roles as it is stated in the book *Brave-Hearted Women: Images of Lakota Women from the Pine Ridge Reservation, South Dakota.* Because of the commercial success of *Dances with Wolves,* one of the few Hollywood movies ever to come close to a Native point of view, the Lakota people are in the public consciousness again. Yet the roles of the women in *Dances with Wolves* are sometime so subtle that I am afraid all too many people see the movie with eyes that only take in the dealings of men with men. In *Brave-Hearted Women,* Margaret Hawk, a Lakota elder, says this:

> In the old days, the women were the teachers, so my mother and my grandmother were my teachers. ... I remember my grandma saying: "Don't go through the fire. You're going to get burned and there are ways to go around it."
>
> She also taught me the Lakota tradition of how to live. There were the four cardinal virtues: bravery, honesty, generosity and fortitude for men; modesty and chastity also for women.[9]

In the introduction to that same book, Carolyn Reyer sums up the roles of Lakota men and women:

> In Sioux society the men were the protectors, the providers; the women were the homemakers. Unfortunately, popular literature and films have distorted the role of women by depicting them as slaves and household drudges, unequal or inferior to

their men. This is far from the truth. The Lakota woman was a total individual, and her "physical, spiritual, emotional and mental makeup was not derived from the Lakota male. She had her own name suited to her personality and ability and did not take her father's or husband's name."[10]

When I am asked how these traditions of balance affect masculinity, my first response is always to say that true masculinity is strengthened. Any role which depends upon its continuation by the domination of another group by a rule of force (whether it be the force of tradition or mere brute force) is a role which will always be threatened. When masculinity means dictatorship, there is always the danger of overthrow. Dictatorial regimes sow the seeds of their own destruction—as events in the early 1990s in Russia have shown the world. But when your role is that of a person in partnership with others, the weight upon your shoulders is lessened in many ways. Men and women are meant to work together, like two hands. One of the stories found among the Navajo in their *Dine Bahane* (the long Navajo Creation story) tells of the time when the men and women quarreled and separated from each other, living on opposite sides of a stream. Their reconciliation came when they realized that neither sex could live a full life without the other.

Women, Native traditions tell us, are natural teachers. One only has to observe the relation of a healthy child (male or female) and a healthy mother to see how much learning takes place and how central that learning relationship is to human development. Men who acknowledge this role of women as teachers not only learn more themselves, they may also become better teachers in their own ways. We see this in certain Native child-rearing practices which appear to be universal across the continent and which I have attempted to follow with my own sons. We are taught—women and men alike—that we should not strike our children. Men and women alike are encouraged to show love and approval to their children. Accounts, too numerous to mention, can be found written by Europeans amazed at the way "fierce Indian warriors" behaved with their own small children, frequently kissing them and showing them great tenderness. Such behavior toward his sons, in particular, by a man is often called "womanish" by contemporary white Americans or is called "spoiling your child." Yet to the Native peoples, to the best of my knowledge, no one—adult or child—can ever be spoiled by too much love and approval given in the proper way.

When children do wrong, rather than hitting them or physically abusing them, the first step toward correction is to tell a lesson story. Traditional stories—such as the Abenaki tale of how Skunk loses his beautiful white fur and becomes bad smelling because he is envious—show the results of bad behavior and it is believed that such lessons remain in the child's heart, even though the child may not know it at the time. It is said that physically abusing a child can break that child's spirit. Physical abuse is regarded as a bad example, too. It is not brave to beat someone who is much smaller than yourself, but if you do it to your children, they will do the same to smaller children and, eventually, to their own children. It is also a practical thing, not to abuse your children. One day in your old age, when you are the one who is small and weak, how will your children treat you? My wife Carol and I have two grown sons, both of whom are now much bigger and stronger than I am. Not only does it make me feel proud when I hear them described as "gentle giants," it also makes me feel a lot more secure about my own survival!

A man may be the one chosen by one Native tradition or another (remember, when we speak of Native Americans or American Indians we are talking about more than four hundred different cultures spanning a wide continent) to stand up and speak in council—but a woman's voice is just as strong, and when a man speaks with the voices of the women supporting him, his words have special power.

In the summer of 1990 I attended the Traditional Circle of Elders, a gathering of Native elders from many tribal nations all over the American continent held each year. The Circle was at Onondaga, the Iroquois Nation which acts as the "fire keepers" for the Iroquois Confederacy. (The present-day city of Syracuse, New York, is at the edge of Onondaga territory. In fact, a big part of Syracuse is on land still owned by the Onondagas and leased to the city.) One of the chiefs stood up to show the assembled Native elders one of the Iroquois wampum belts. Those wampum belts are made of shell beads strung to form patterns which signify treaties or special relations between nations. Some are hundreds of years old and they are only brought out on very special occasions. The wampum belt was in a glass case to protect it and he held it out before him so the other elders could see it, gravely telling its special meaning. It was a moment charged with power and dignity, and people seemed very moved by his eloquence. However, when he paused to take a breath, one of the Clan Mothers spoke up from the back of the circle.

"You're holding it upside down," she said, in a voice which was both gentle and firm.

The laughter which came then, from all of us and from the Chief (as he quickly turned the case), was not laughter at another's expense but a laughter of recognition—recognition that the serious is balanced by the humorous, recognition of the power of women and the teaching role which they hold. It was also a wonderful, subtle example of the ways in which men's and women's roles complement and strengthen each other within Iroquois culture. Just as in the past, it is the Clan Mother who watches what the Chief does in public and makes sure that he does it properly. Because she could see from her perspective what he could not see from his, the two of them together were able to make it right.

For the original Native cultures of what we now call America, it seems feminism may have a different meaning. The vision of women is not an alternative to dominant male thought; it is an equal force, a force which shapes the thoughts and the lives of everyone, teaching the deepest values. Real men are strengthened by the strength of women. Together we can make a balance as powerful and sustaining as that of Earth and Sky.

Notes

1. Governor Edward Winslow, "Account of the Natives of New England," in *New England's Memorial,* Nathaniel Morton, ed. (Boston: Congregational Board of Publications, 1855), 486–494.
2. Christopher Levette, "A Voyage into New England," in *Collections*, 3rd Series, 8 (Boston: Massachusetts Historical Society, 1843).
3. Howard S. Russell, *Indian New England before the Mayflower* (Hanover, NH: University Press of New England, 1980), 96–97.
4. Roger Williams, *Complete Writings,* vol. I (New York: Russell and Russell, 1963), 123.
5. Will Roscoe, *The Zuni Man-Woman* (Albuquerque: University of New Mexico Press, 1991).
6. James E. Seaver, *A Narrative of the Life of Mrs. Mary Jemison* (Syracuse, NY: Syracuse University Press, 1990).
7. Marilou Awiakta, *Selu: Seeking the Corn-Mother's Wisdom* (Golden, CO: Fulcrum Publishing, 1993).
8. Leo Bonfanti, *Biographies and Legends of the New England Indians* (Wakefield, MA: Pride Publications, 1968).
9. Carolyn Reyer, *Cante Ohitika Win (Brave-Hearted Women),* additional writing by Dr. Bea Medicine and Debra Lynn White Plume (Vermillion: University of South Dakota Press, 1991), 16.
10. Ibid., 5.

SPEAKING AGAIN TO THE DEER

❂

In much of my writing I draw on my knowledge of Native American cultures—especially Abenaki (my own Native heritage) and Iroquois—and on the experiences of growing up and continuing to live in the Adirondack Mountain region of northern New York State. More so than perhaps any other poem I have written, *The Deer Are Calling Us* weaves together those two deep roots of my writing.

▲▼▲

My father was a taxidermist and, therefore, a man very familiar with the death of animals. He was also a good hunter, not only in the sense of being successful when he hunted, but also in the sense of having a special respect for the animals he hunted—especially deer. The thought of wasting any part of an animal he killed disturbed him. I remember how when hunters brought in the heads and skins of deer they had killed, he would skin out the neck so that we could use the meat for making venison stews.

▲▼▲

Each autumn would find him hunting along the ridges above the Hudson and Cedar Rivers near the town of Indian Lake—which was named for the Abenaki guides who lived there. Although people often thought my father was American Indian—his hair was thick and black, his skin dark, his eyes slanted, his cheekbones high—he was actually Slovak. The Indian blood was on my mother's side. Despite being Slovak, my father's life was always deeply influenced by Indian ways. His first partner and teacher, Leon Pray, was an elderly American Indian and when my father had a near-fatal heart attack at the age of seventy, he told me that he had seen Mr. Pray, who was waiting for him in a place where they would always be able to hunt and fish together.

▲▼▲

Among the Native people of the Northeast, there is a strong understanding that the human beings are neither wiser nor more important than the animal people. The deer, it is said, may appear to take the form of humans when they are in their own villages, and there are stories of a hunter finding a strange village in the forest, staying there for some time and then, upon leaving and looking back, seeing the village fade away as deer run back into the forest. Only then does he realize that he was the guest of the Deer People.

▲▼▲

The deer are as important to the Native people of the Northeast Woodlands as the buffalo is to the Native people of the Great Plains. When a good hunter enters the forest, he hunts because he needs the meat and skins of the deer to help his people survive, and he shows the deer respect when he hunts them. He offers them a gift of tobacco and says thank you to their spirits when he kills a deer. Because of this, the deer allow him to kill them. But if he does not show the proper respect, he will be unsuccessful or may even be injured or killed while hunting.

▲▼▲

The figure of the Deer Woman is encountered again and again in contemporary Native American stories. She can be a very dangerous being and may be seeking revenge, some say, for the modern mistreatment of the animals and the earth by humans. In one story a lovely young woman appears at a dance and almost succeeds in drawing a young man away with her. But when she lifts up her long dress, he sees that she has the hooves of a deer and escapes from her.

▲▼▲

In *The Deer Are Calling Us* I have tried to both tell a story and, in the old sense of traditional thanksgiving prayers, acknowledge again the importance of the deer and the spiritual relationship which we, as human beings, must maintain with the living world around us, a world constantly sacrificing parts of itself to ensure our survival.

The Deer Are Calling Us

The deer are calling us
I look into the hills
and I see them in the grey place there
where the line of trees and the stone
of the hillside become one with sky
We are not a dream, they say.
We have been waiting.

We know you and
the name of your family.

Every year for more than half a century
my father walked into hills like these
to kill the deer with guns that he loved.

I do not know how many times
I helped him
drag their bodies down slopes.
Perhaps it was many times, perhaps
it was only once that I bent
to loop a piece of rope about the horns
and drag the deer back to the camp
pain between my shoulders
as the stiffening body
wore a trail through leaves and snow
before it was hung from the pole in the shed.
Perhaps I am still there, a boy
struggling with the weight
of death at the end of a rope.

My father killed
at least one deer
for every year he walked
this earth
and still the old

understanding remained, never spoken
to men he hunted beside.
The deer he killed were his brothers.

We're ready to die for you
they said and he answered them

They do not speak
those words to me,
yet wherever I travel
some part of the deer
goes with me
the grey skin case
of my drum, the buckskin shirt,
the moccasins on my feet,
the string
of braided leather around my neck.
As a child, eating
the meat of the deer
I felt them become
a part of me
they made my body,
my sinew and my bones.
I have held the antlers
of slain deer as many times
as I've held the hands of friends.

My sons have never killed a deer,
though they have learned
to walk close enough
to touch a deer, wild in the forest,
and I will not kill a deer again.
Yet the tracks of deer circle our house
and their eyes follow my passage each time
I walk along forest trails as familiar to me
as the streets of a city are to other men.

Each autumn men
who do not live close to the forest
walk into the hills.
They follow the trails
and the tracks of the deer
and as they follow, deer spirits are around
them
they think they hear the rippling of water
from the streams that flow
but it is the feet of the deer spirits walking
they think they are touched by wind
but it is the breath of the deer on their faces
if they put down their guns
and let the fallen leaves embrace them,
let the snow shape itself about them
then a deer woman comes
in the shape of a woman
with eyes more beautiful than any dream
they have ever had before
and leads them, leads them
not over the hills, but into the land.

Sometimes, as one of those men
lays down his gun
and lays down his body
to go with the deer woman
a sudden realization
comes to him, quick
as the silver glint of the rising sun
on ice held by a ledge of stone,
that the search parties
will look for him
in vain and as he looks back
he sees his own bones
and the rags of his clothes
will wait for the crows
in the rain.

To follow the deer
you must fear the deer
without being afraid
of your own death.

The roads which cut through the mountains
the trucks which roar the night
the airplanes which rise up above the earth
as if gravity could not hold them
they are all brief illusions to the spirits of deer
waiting for the engines to end,
waiting for roads to break like dark ice,
for all to fall that must fall.

The deer are calling us,
calling us back into the forest,
back into the hills that remember men
who have forgotten them,
who have forgotten our survival
is a thread of breath,
sad men who have forgotten
those who kill
must know how to pray.

An Unbroken Circle

✦

"There are no more traditional Iroquois storytellers." Those were the words once spoken to me in 1970 by a scholar whose life's work focussed on the Iroquois. It was an interesting statement, for it defined not only a whole group of people who had for untold centuries held a central role in the lives of the Haudenosaunee, it also extinguished, from that point on, the legitimacy of anyone claiming to be an "Iroquois storyteller." In a way, it was typical of the attitude toward storytelling in America in general. Storytelling belongs to a vanished past, a past that has no place in a fast-moving modern world.

I didn't say anything then in response to that statement, especially when it was followed by that same speaker's assertion that he had known the very last traditional Iroquois storyteller and that person had died some twenty years ago. When such statements are made, it isn't easy—or even advisable—to answer quickly. Now that a quarter century has passed, I think I'm almost ready to make an answer.

I am not a folklorist, an anthropologist, an ethnologist or an Iroquois expert. I'm not an Iroquois (though, I've been told by some who fall into these categories that being an Iroquois automatically disqualifies one from eligibility as—to put it in legal parlance—an expert witness for the defense). Therefore, I probably do not have the proper vocabulary to resurrect that scientifically interred group of people called "traditional Iroquois storytellers." With the right vocabulary, you can define anything out of existence—even yourself. However, like the bumblebee who buzzes blithely from flower to flower despite the fact that careful scientific study once showed it is totally unable to fly because of faulty aerodynamics, I may be too uninformed to allow logic to get in the way of my own flight.

Instead, I intend to talk about what I consider to be the unbroken circle of Iroquois storytelling on the basis of my experience, not as a student of Iroquois culture, but as a writer and a storyteller who has been listening for the greater part of his half century on this earth to living Iroquois people telling stories. My view of storytelling, therefore, is on the level of experience rather than academic study.

In a small way, it is like the difference between traditional education in the Native sense and the traditions of education in the Western sense. In a western education, when you desire to learn something, you apply for admission to a school, pay a lot of money over a period of years, sign up for classes, listen to lectures, take notes, study for tests and accumulate grade points. At the end of it all, you are given a piece of paper with your name and a few letters on it—B.A., M.A., Ph.D. In a traditional education, in the Native sense, if you want to learn something—basket making, let's say—then you go to a basket maker whose work you admire. You hang around watching and helping that person out. Over the years, by doing, you learn how and when to gather the right materials and your hands get the feel of basket making. At the end of the process—though the "end" is not so clearly defined here—you are able to make baskets. Didactic versus experiential. Two different ways of learning and seeing the world. I don't want to say that one is inherently superior to the other (unless you need an actual basket in which to carry something), but I do think that it may be the difference between these two ways of learning and experiencing the world which has made it easier for non-Native "experts" to close the book on certain aspects of Native cultures which (to continue that metaphor) are still being written. Then again, the metaphor of "closing a book" isn't appropriate for a culture which values oral tradition. Oral tradition is not easily seen and thus can be kept hidden. It is something which can only be remembered by those who know how to listen and spoken only by those who have listened for a long time. And everything I am about to write from this point on is based on what I have heard, thus far—even though I am still listening.

▲▼▲

Storytelling, among the Haudenosaunee as among the other Native nations of North America, has always served *at least* two major functions. One of those functions is to entertain. It is important that a story is entertaining, even entrancing, for a number of reasons. An interesting story is easier to remember. An entertaining story takes one out of the present moment into something which might be called the eternal or the mythic. (I use these terms which do not exist in Iroquois or most other Native languages because, in English, they may make some sense to the reader. The term *wahon:nise* in Mohawk, which translates roughly as "a long time ago," may make more sense in an Iroquois context.) When you consider the fact that these stories were told during the cold months of the year when life may have been very difficult for the people, it may be easier to recognize the value of being taken out of the present moment, not so much to escape as to be given new energy or understanding with which to face that present moment when the story has been told.

The second major function of storytelling is to instruct. Native American cultures, including the Iroquois, were described by early European observers as being cultures "without laws." This, of course, was an oversimplification on the part of outsiders who could not perceive the subtleties of the laws which, indeed, did exist. Rather than lacking laws, Native North American nations tended to rely on laws which were remarkably nonintrusive when compared to the laws of Europe. The idea of *noninterference* is strong throughout Native North America and is still seen clearly today. Native people tend *not* to tell others what they should and shouldn't do. Instead, other indirect mechanisms were used and continue to be used to inform individuals when they overstepped the social boundaries. Joking and teasing might be used to remind someone of their place in societies—such as that of the Haudenosaunee—which place great value on equality. Storytelling is one of the strongest methods of such instruction. Because Native people did not believe in striking children to discipline them, stories were a very important way of pointing out to an erring child what might happen to one whose actions cause trouble for others. (My own Abenaki grandfather told me how his father would never hit him when he did wrong. Instead, he said, his father would talk to him and tell him stories. "And them stories," my grandfather said, "was strong! Sometimes I wished my father would hit me instead of telling me them stories!")

One marvelous example of such a lesson story can be found in the 1976 collection *Kanien'keha' Okara'Shon:'a* ("Mohawk Stories") which was published as Bulletin 427 by the New York State Museum. The stories in the collection are all in bilingual format, Mohawk and English, and are contemporary in that they were written down by living Mohawk people who knew these stories as part of their own traditions. Any number of the stories in the book could be described as lesson stories, appropriate for use in disciplining a child, but my favorite is the one Mae Montour says was told to her by her own father, Louis T. Curotte. It is called *Akon:Wara'*. *Akon:Wara'* is a monster whose name means "Ugly Face." He is especially fond of taking disobedient children. In Mae Montour's version, a grandmother is left with her grandchildren who are misbehaving. After warning them that she will give them to Ugly Face if they do not behave, she thrusts one of them outside, shouts *Koh akon:wara' ki:ken raksa:'a* ("Here, Ugly Face, take this boy!") and slams the door. A little while passes, and she opens the door to let the child in. However, the boy is gone and is never seen again. The lessons in this story cut more than one way. It is not only a story which cautions children to behave; it reminds elders to be aware of the consequences of their own actions when they discipline the young.

Such monsters, which are a natural curb to the disrespectful or dangerous actions of young children, are found throughout the Native world. Unlike parental rules which may not be enforced when the parents are not around, the monsters of the stories never sleep. And the children listen! I've done workshops in storytelling in Native schools throughout the United States and I always enjoy the results I get when I ask the young people to tell me monster stories. A few of them, of course, may talk about Freddy Kruger or a character out of some TV show, but the really scary monsters are always those which really do exist out there. In a third-grade class in the Akwesasne Mohawk School, some years ago, I heard several versions of the "underwater wolverine" story, the tale of a monster who lurks under the thin ice of the St. Lawrence River, waiting to pull in unwary children who venture out too far. "You can tell he's there," one child said, "when you see the bubbles under the ice!" (A good sign that the ice is, in fact, too thin to walk on.) It was a tale which reminded me of the Toad Woman of Abenaki stories, who drowns children foolish enough to venture into the truly dangerous cedar bogs alone. (There is some similarity in such stories, of course, to such European tales as Little Red Riding Hood and Hansel and Gretel. Perhaps these European tales also had the original purpose of teaching children to avoid dangerous situations by frightening them. Such cautionary stories are found all over the world. However, the practical teaching value of such European folktales has largely been lost and they are usually viewed as nothing more than children's stories. Further, those European folktales of monsters are not balanced by other stories—as are those in Native American traditions—which present the natural world in a more positive light. In European storytelling traditions, the forests are to be cut down and nature is meant to be conquered, not respected and understood.) Somehow, though the "last traditional Iroquois storyteller" had died decades before these kids were born, the traditional stories were still reaching them in a highly effective way.

Having defined certain traditional uses of Iroquois stories—as I understand them—perhaps it is time to talk about just what is meant by a "traditional Iroquois storyteller." In his 1923 publication *Seneca Myths and Folk Tales* (reprinted in 1989 by the University of Nebraska with an introduction by William Fenton), Arthur C. Parker, whose father was Seneca, gives a classic description of such a person. In his introduction Parker says: "A storyteller was known as *'hage'ota'* and his stock of stories called *'ganondas'hagon.'* Each listener gave the storyteller a small gift, as a bead, small round brooch, beads, tobacco, or other trinket. To tell stories was called *'ansege'oden,'* and the gift was called *'dagwa'niatcis,'* now an obsolete word." Parker then describes in the chapter "The Atmosphere of Stories" the appearance of such a *hage'ota'* with his *gustoweh* cap topped by an eagle feather and his bag filled with trophies "to remind him of his stories—bear teeth, shells, bark dolls, strings of wampum. ..."

Parker's book is a useful, informative volume. If we are to limit the definition of a "traditional Iroquois storyteller" to someone who looks, lives and acts exactly as Parker's *hage'ota'* does in his storytelling vignette, then there are, indeed, no more Iroquois storytellers. If outward and easily perceived appearance is to be the measure of any human institution, then we can just as easily apply these standards to almost any aspect of any human culture and declare it extinct by saying it isn't exactly the same as it was "back then." Such standards of judgment are being constantly used against Native people—and not just by certain social scientists. Witness the federal government's efforts in recent years with the Wampanoags and other native nations who have been told that they do not, by government definition, "exist as a tribe." (To show how crazy that can get, a federal jury using criteria established by a federal judge actually decided that the Wampanoags of Mashpee were a tribe in 1834 and 1842, but not in 1790, 1870 and 1976.)

What then, by my own "loose" definition, constitutes an Iroquois storyteller today? Well, it is obviously not someone playing exactly the same role as the *hage'ota'* of yesteryear. Those men, usually of middle age, would travel from longhouse to longhouse telling stories and being given presents for their efforts. I do not think, I should quickly say, that traditional storytelling was ever limited to a small class of middle-aged men. I firmly believe that folklorists will agree with me when I say that traditional storytelling is also deeply rooted in families. The stories passed down from generation to generation within a family still exist. Today, sometimes they are told in English to the children, but in a great many homes—Seneca, Onondaga, Tuscarora, Mohawk, Oneida and Cayuga homes—those stories are still being told in the original Iroquois languages. Daniel Thompson, who writes and paints under the name Rokwaho, told me about the stories his own father used to tell in Mohawk, stories which he now passes on to the next generation. Mae Montour's Ugly Face story, learned from her father, is another example. However, in addition to those continuing family storytelling traditions, there are, in fact, a number of people out there in the world who are carrying on their storytelling practice in a way remarkably similar to the old *hage'ota'*. Not only are they going from "longhouse to longhouse," they are also going outside the longhouse into the non-Indian world. Oren Lyons (Jo ag quis ho), an Onondaga Faithkeeper, carries a number of traditional messages with him around the world as an ambassador of the Iroquois people and the Onondaga Nation, and his ability as a storyteller is one of the reasons he is so effective. Jake Swamp, of the Mohawk Nation, travels all over the world, planting Trees of Peace and telling the story of the coming of the Peacemaker. He doesn't do this for pay but accepts donations to pay his expenses. Both Oren and Jake, clearly, are aware of the two roles of storytelling I outlined earlier in this essay. Audrey Shenandoah (Gonwaianni) combines the roles of being a Clan Mother with teaching Onondaga language and culture in the Onondaga Indian School, making continual use of storytelling in her classes and when she is called upon to speak in public.

There are, in fact, a number of types of traditional storytelling still to be found among the Iroquois. There are family stories, including cautionary tales told to the young and tales which are full-blown myths and legends in the folkloric sense of the words. There are ghost stories, many of which take place in present time. DuWayne Bowen is a contemporary Seneca storyteller who has been hearing (I hesitate to use the word "collecting" because it implies the kind of coming into a community for a few weeks each year, recording and then scramming, which has characterized some of the interactions between Natives and their non-Native observers for the past century) such contemporary ghost stories for years. In 1990 Bowen put down on paper a number of the tales he had heard over the years. These were published by the Greenfield Review Press under the title *One More Story.*

There are stories of things which have happened in everyday life which easily fit the category of storytelling. Ted C. Williams, who is Tuscarora, is known for *The Reservation,* his collection of such stories about life on the Tuscarora Reservation, near Niagara Falls, when he was growing up. Having heard Ted before an audience, I know that he could easily fill up another book or two with such tales and he, too, has been listening to and remembering contemporary Indian ghost stories for two decades.

Then there are the great cycles of tales to be told at public gatherings which may take several days in the telling or may be told in brief. The story of the coming of the Peacemaker is one such cycle. Its story tells of a time when the Iroquois Nations were engaged in bloody internecine warfare. They had forgotten the original instructions given them long ago by the Creator. Tom Porter, who is Mohawk, explained to me that peace and respect were at the heart of those original instructions. Giving thanks was one of the most important parts of the ceremonies. But the people had forgotten respect and forgotten how to give thanks. Instead, they thought only of revenge. In that world, which is poignantly familiar to those of us who listen to newscasts filled with endless reports of ethnic cleansing and reprisal raids, there was no peace. So the Creator sent down a messenger to teach the people the meaning of peace once again. That man became known as the Peacemaker. As Oren Lyons explained a few years ago at the Onondaga Nation School when he told part of the story of the Peacemaker, "This story can be told long or short. And every part of this story has other stories connected to it."

Because the Haudenosaunee are alive as a people and, like all people, growing and changing, there are new cycles of tales coming into being.

The great story of Handsome Lake is a recent epic cycle, one given to the people through divine revelation less than two centuries ago. It is another story with modern reverberations. Handsome Lake, one of the chiefs of the Iroquois, was dying of alcoholism and despair. It was 1800, not long after the Iroquois people had found themselves cheated of much of their land following the Revolutionary War. It seemed as if, to many observers, the Iroquois people were doomed to die out. Then, while in an alcoholic coma—seemingly dead—Handsome Lake was visited by divine messengers. They took him to the Sky Land and showed him many things—a giant woman grasping at everything around her and unable to stand—the embodiment of greed; an evil being bringing a deadly drink to the people—the alcohol which was killing so many. They showed him many such sights and, explaining them, gave him a message, a good message. The Iroquois must cease drinking. They must again respect elders and children. They must care for their crops and be faithful to their husbands and wives. They must accept certain aspects of Western culture, but remain Longhouse People in their hearts. Handsome Lake was told to remember all that he saw in the Sky Land and to deliver it as a message to his people. That message saved not only the life of Handsome Lake, but transformed the destiny of the Iroquois. It was a story which helped them survive. To this day the *Gai'wi'io* of *Ganio'dai'io,* the "Good Message of Handsome Lake," is spoken in the longhouses. Its length is such that it takes several days to deliver the epic story.

Those who have learned the "Good Message" and whose telling of it meets set standards in the eyes of the elders, such people as Jake Thomas, a Cayuga chief from the Six Nations Reserve, deliver the sacred story cycle at a certain time of the year, going from one Iroquois Nation's longhouse to the next.

Because of the current growing national interest in storytelling as a performance art, there is great demand for Native stories. Iroquois tales are being told to appreciative audiences by both non-Iroquois tellers who have attempted to learn the stories in the right way from Native people and even by an increasing number of Iroquois people themselves who are trying their hands at being "professional storytellers." If you make a summer visit to the Six Nations Indian Museum in Onchiota, New York, you will find either the Mohawk elder, Ray Fadden

(Tehanetorens), or his son, John (Kahionhes), using beaded record belts to tell traditional Mohawk tales. Ray's nephew, Steven Fadden, has gained a reputation not only as a scholar whose writings about Iroquois culture and tradition have been widely published, but as a storyteller himself, performing at schools and storytelling festivals. In western New York, there are such fine Seneca storytellers as Marion Miller and Charlene Winger. Perhaps, twenty years from now, some of those people will no longer be walking among us, but there will be others to take their place. In many ways, storytelling among the Iroquois today is alive and well.

It is important to recognize the Native understanding that stories have a life of their own and that stories may be given to a person or to a nation as a whole. The first stories, according to one Seneca tale, were given to a boy by a giant boulder. Stories, it seems, come from the earth itself. To assume that the passing of a certain way of life or the disappearance of a certain group of people within a nation would mean the breaking of the circle, and the complete disappearance of the sorts of traditional stories they told, just doesn't make sense. Even without the people, the stories are still out there, alive, waiting to be heard. The Iroquois storytellers of today remember one of the most important things we can all do as human beings. That thing is to keep our ears open. Listen for the songs still held by that unbroken circle, the life of the world all around us. Listen for the stories that teach us. Listen for the stories of respect and peace.

PART II

STORYTELLING AND THE SACRED

Why the People Speak Many Languages

(A Seneca Story)

Long ago, when the earth was new, all of the people spoke a single language. The people lived in peace and harmony then. They shared everything that they had and they had everything which anyone could ever need. They grew corn and beans and squash in their fields. They hunted the game animals in the forest. They gave thanks to the earth and the food plants, to the animals, and to their great Creator who had provided everything in such abundance.

In those days, in the big village by the wide river, there lived a woman chief. Her name was Godasiyo and she was a good chief. She was wise and generous and did everything she could to make the lives of her people peaceful and filled with harmony. There were so many people that the village was located on both sides of the wide river. Although the people did not know how to use boats in those days, they had built a strong bridge across the river. They had tied trees and branches together and woven them in such a way that it was easy for people to walk back and forth from one side to the other. This the people did often, for on the western bank of the river, dances were held each night. There the people would come and bring whatever they had to trade. Some would bring skins and herbs from the forest. Some would bring dried corn or berries from the fields. Whatever was needed could always be gotten either in trade or as a gift, for if anyone truly wanted something but had nothing to trade in exchange, that man or woman had only to say "Brother, I have need of that," or "Sister, would you give that to me?" Then they would be given whatever it was that they needed.

One day, though, something happened. In those days, the people had many dogs. The small white dog which lived in the lodge of Godasiyo, which was on the western bank of the wide stream, had puppies. This had happened before and, as was the custom, whenever a dog had puppies they would be treated as members of the family, and anyone who wished to adopt one of those new little ones had only to ask. This time, however, something was different. One of the four puppies in the litter was as white as its brothers, but it had two dark spots over its eyes. It looked as if it had four eyes. Such dogs are said to be wiser and better than all others, able to see things with those two spots over their eyes which make them great hunters and natural leaders. That little dog was so special that Godasiyo decided to keep it for herself. Thus the trouble began.

Soon the people on the western bank began to brag about the special dog which their chief had in her lodge.

"It is a dog like no other," they said.

"None of the people on the eastern bank of the wide stream have such a special dog in their lodges," they boasted.

It was the first time that such boasting had been heard in Big Village. Soon, something else appeared in Big Village. That something was envy. The people on the eastern bank began to envy their brothers and sisters who had such a special dog on their side of the stream.

Though Godasiyo was a very wise chief, at first she did not see what was happening. Then, one day, a group of people from her side of the village came to her.

"We are worried," they said. "Those bad people on the other side of the stream are talking about our four-eyed dog. We think they may try to steal our dog. We must make ready to fight them!"

Godasiyo was shocked. How could her people fight each other. She walked among them and listened and looked and she saw how bad things had become. The people were divided and none of her words could bring them back together again. She thought of allowing the people on the eastern bank to take the little four-eyed dog. Then she saw that it would only bring the jealousy over to the western side. The people on both sides were now making weapons and Godasiyo knew she had to act. She gathered together the people on the western bank and told them what to do.

"Destroy the bridge," she said.

They did as she said, setting fire to the bridge. Now the people were divided. But Godasiyo knew that another bridge might be built and that fighting might still happen.

"We must leave this place," she said. She had watched the way the pieces of wood from the bridge floated away as they fell into the water and she had an idea. She told the people to gather big pieces of bark from the birch trees and to sew them together in the same way they made baskets and cooking pots of bark. Then, using pitch to seal the seams, the people made the first canoes. They made a number of small canoes and also two very big canoes. The canoes were enough to hold all of the people on the western side of the river.

Then the people made ready to leave for a new place where they could find peace and harmony. But as soon as they started to get into the canoes trouble began again. The people began to argue about which canoe would be the special canoe which would carry their chief and her wonderful four-eyed dog!

Was there no end of this quarreling? Godasiyo felt very tired and sad. But she had another idea.

"We will tie saplings between the two big canoes," she said. Then, in the middle, we will make a platform. My dog and I will ride on that platform. That way we will not be in either canoe and there can be no jealousy."

So it was that they set out and all went well until they came to a place where the river divided into two channels. There, once again, the people began to quarrel. Those in the canoes to the right wanted to take the eastern channel. Those in the canoes to the left wanted to take the western channel. Godasiyo tried to stop them, but they did not listen to her. The people began to turn their canoes in the two different directions and those in the two big canoes, which had Godasiyo's platform suspended between them, also disagreed about which way to go. The lead paddlers in each of the two big canoes called for their people to paddle harder so they would pull the other canoe toward their side. As they struggled back and forth, the two canoes pulled apart and the platform holding Godasiyo and the little four-eyed dog fell into the river.

The people leaned over the side of their canoes and looked down into the water. Their chief and the little dog had vanished. In their places were a big sturgeon and a little white fish. As the people watched in wonder, the fish swam away.

The people tried then to speak to each other about what had happened. But they could no longer understand each other. Jealousy and quarreling had divided the people. Those in each canoe spoke different languages. So the people separated and continued on their way. Each time the rivers divided, the people split again and more languages came into the world. So it is to this day.

Note: A version of this tale, entitled "The Legend of Godasiyo," was collected in the autumn of 1896, by the Tuscarora Indian ethnologist J. N. B. Hewitt. It was published as part of the book *Seneca Fiction, Legends, and Myths,* collected by Jeremiah Curtin and J. N. B. Hewitt in 1899 as the 32nd Annual Report of the Bureau of American Ethnology. My own version of this tale draws on the Hewitt telling, though it differs in some details. An earlier version of my retelling, slightly different from this one, can be found in my book *Return of the Sun* (Crossing Press), 1990. Though I have heard versions of it from Iroquois friends in English, the story was given originally to Hewitt in Seneca. I mention this because people have remarked to me on the similarity of this tale to the story of the Tower of Babel from the Old Testament. Some have asked if this story really is an authentic Indian tale because of this similarity.

In many ways, though, this is a very different story. It presents a world in which peace and harmony are the natural order of things. It is only the introduction of jealousy and bragging which break that natural order. Among the Iroquois people of the Northeast, peace is still greatly valued. The five original Iroquois Nations—Mohawk, Oneida, Onondaga, Cayuga and Seneca—were brought together a thousand years ago into a League of Peace after many years of bloody warfare. The peace was brought to them by a special messenger from the Creator named the Peacemaker. The Peacemaker joined forces with a wise elderly woman named Jigonsaseh and a great orator named Hiawatha. Together they united the people and planted a great pine tree as the symbol of their peaceful union. Later, those five Iroquois Nations were joined by the Tuscarora. The leaders of the Iroquois Great League had to be men of peace and could not serve as delegates to the Great League as "chiefs," if they went to war. To this day, the Iroquois chiefs speak for peace. Such men as Chief Oren Lyons of the Onondaga Nation and Chief Jake Swamp of the Mohawk Nation have taken the Iroquois message of peace throughout the world from the many nations of Europe to Australia. Decades ago, an Iroquois leader from the Tuscarora, Clinton Rickard, spoke of peace and Native rights to the League of Nations. Despite our many languages, when we stop quarreling and begin to talk of peace, we find that we can understand each other once again.

Opening the Wind

Our eyes hold more of the world than we think we see. Our ears are open to more songs than we think we have heard. Two decades ago, a Cherokee botanist and poet named Norman Russell told me about a way of learning how to listen which was given to him by his father. He called it "Opening the Wind."

Like many of the old teachings, it is not hard to describe. In only a few words, he explained to me what it meant and how it could be done. But, like looking into your own heart, it is something easier described than done. Since that day I have been trying, at times with some success, to follow that teaching. I've passed it on to my own children. Like our old stories, it seems simple on the surface. But once you listen deeply, you realize that it has many levels. As often as I tell any of our traditional tales, there still comes a time when I realize that there is something more about that story than I had realized. It is that way with anything which is carried on the breath. Stories, life, wind.

This is how you can begin to open the wind.

Find a place where you can sit quietly away from other people. It doesn't have to be deep in the forest or on a mountaintop. It can be on a back porch. Choose a warm summer evening to try this for the first time. When the light begins to fade, our eyes turn inward and our ears are ready to be opened.

Now imagine a circle around yourself. That circle is no wider than your outstretched arms. Close your eyes and listen to all that you can hear within that circle. Concentrate on that circle. At first you may find it hard to hear anything distinct. Be patient. You will hear the sound of your own breathing. Listen closely and relax as you listen. You may hear the rustle of your clothes or your feet moving on the floor. Relax, move if you feel a need to, but sit as still as possible. Perhaps now you will hear the creak of the floorboards under your feet, perhaps you will begin to hear the sound of your own heart.

Other sounds from further away will begin to intrude upon you. Don't worry about them. You'll reach out for them later. Know that they are there, but concentrate on the close sounds first. When you feel you have done this long enough—and how long you do this is up to you, no exact timing or clocks are needed—open your eyes. See if you can identify sounds that you heard but did not recognize.

Now, imagine that circle being much larger. Perhaps you might make it twice as large. Close your eyes and listen again. You do not have to forget about the first sounds that you heard. Those will still be there. Just accept them and then move beyond them. Listen patiently and enjoy the sounds that you hear. You may hear the sound of a cricket singing. You may hear the rustle of the wind in the leaves. Of course, if you are in a city, it may seem hard to hear those natural sounds. Sirens and voices, the roar and rumble of traffic, all seem to blot everything out. Even neon lights make their own distinctive humming sounds as the filaments within them glow and burn. But if you listen, really listen, you will hear other things that were not noticed before. Sitting on a rooftop in New York City, I began to hear a new sound one night. That sound was a steady, repeated call, almost like a *Bee-eep,* a call that circled around and above me. It was a nightjar, a nocturnal bird, circling as it hunted for insects. Its nest was in one corner of that same Manhattan rooftop.

Once again, open your eyes. Perhaps you will want to go no farther than this on your first night. You may find that listening to those first two circles, taking those first two steps to open the wind, took you only a few minutes by clock time. Or, if you were patient and allowed that listening to become part of the rhythm of your breath, you may find that hours have passed.

Even if you think your hearing is not particularly good, you may be surprised at all you hear when you concentrate in this way. You keep enlarging your circles as you listen further. You may begin to hear sounds from a hundred yards away—or even further. One night, as I listened closely, I heard a sound that I could not identify. I opened my eyes and looked for that dog I heard faintly barking. Finally, I got out my bicycle and rode along the side of the darkened road. I rode until I stood in front of the place where that dog was still barking from inside, its paws up against the window of a house more than a mile away from my own.

Once you have begun to learn how to open the wind, which also teaches you how to separate sounds from each other and locate their source, you may find yourself able to do some interesting things. It is, for example, possible to be in a place full of people who are talking and focus your hearing on conversations taking place on the other side of the room. But, best of all, opening the wind can prepare you to hear and appreciate the sounds of the world around you. I think of the day when my father and I went out on a boat in Deer Pond in the heart of the Adirondack Mountains. As we paddled out, three loons flew up and began to circle the pond. I closed my eyes and listened. Not only could I hear their wing beats, I could hear how the wing beats of each of those three big birds were not the same. Each bird's wings had its own distinctive sound and I knew, having truly heard them, I would never forget them.

I listened and I am still listening. And as I listen I think again of my friend Norman Russell and thank him—*Wado, wado*—for helping me open the wind.

> Whenever we breathe
> we breathe in a circle.
>
> That circle is endless,
> breathed out, breathed in.
>
> Whenever we breathe,
> we are part of the wind.
> We borrow its voice
> to carry our songs.
>
> We travel on
> that circling wind,
> a circle as old as life.

STORYTELLING AND THE SACRED

❋

*Storytelling is a serious business. It should not be undertaken
thoughtlessly, for if stories should be retold during the growing
season life must come to a halt as the friendly spirits of nature
become enthralled by their magic spell and neglect their appointed
function of providing sustenance for the coming winter. So then
also that part of the spirit which remains and wanders aimlessly
when people die might be enticed into the community when stories
are told, making them long again for the fellowship of the living
and perhaps stealing the spirit of some newborn to keep them
company. People must prepare for stories and youngsters be
protected by a buckskin thong on the wrist to tie them to the world
so they might not be "spirited" away by the dead. Just as many
ceremonies must be postponed until the cold time, so also stories
should be reserved until then.*

—William Guy Spittal, from his Introduction to
Myths of the Iroquois[1]

*On a Northwest reservation I visited, middle-aged Indians told me
that the elders of a certain bent and crippled old man believed that
he had become bent and crippled because of his interviews with a
university student: he had, in 1930, given a stranger information
about his people, and had related tribal tales in the summer.*

—Ella E. Clark, from her Introduction to
Indian Legends from the Northern Rockies[2]

*For the Nez Perce, a legend was more than just an hour's enter-
tainment. Behind the adventures and trials of different heroes and
villains important lessons were always to be found because these
legends were the first formal education a Nez Perce child received.*

By hearing these adventures again and again, the child gathered a great deal of practical information about his own physical surroundings.

... Perhaps the most important lessons to be found in these tales are of a moral nature. To help a child become a good Nez Perce was the main goal of his education. The legends began to teach him, at an early age that his behavior, whether good or bad, had a predictable outcome.

... The legends traditionally were told during the winter season. When a child would ask for a story during the summer, he was told that it was prohibited, or that a snake might come and "visit" his home if he insisted on hearing the stories during the season when food was being gathered and stored for the winter.

—Nu Mee Poom Tit Wah Tit,
Nez Perce Legends by the Nez Perce Tribe of Idaho[3]

It might be supposed that myths and folk-tales which are orally transmitted would suffer great changes as they pass from one storyteller to another, and that in time a given tale would become utterly corrupted, and indeed so changed that it would bear faint resemblance to the "original." Yet an examination of the myths and legends recorded by early observers, such as the early missionaries, show that the modern versions have suffered no essential change. An excellent example is the Iroquoian creation myth, as recorded by the Jesuit fathers in the Relations.

Religious traditions, ceremonies and myths, being of a "sacred" character, must be related with a certain fidelity which forbids any real change in the content. To a lesser degree, perhaps, but not much less, the 'ga'gaa' legends of the Iroquois are protected from violent alteration. The legend is a thing, to the Indian mind, and it has a certain personality. In certain instances the legend is a personal or group possession and its form and content are religiously guarded from change.

—Arthur C. Parker, from his Introduction to
Seneca Myths and Folk Tales[4]

The Storytelling Seasons

Whenever I think of the way stories are passed from one to another, my mind takes me to a certain place and time. I am standing behind the house of Mdawelasis, an Abenaki elder who spent most of his life in the Adirondack town of Old Forge. It is early autumn, not long after the first frost. A basswood log has been stripped of its bark and laid across two sawhorses and the old man is working at it with his carving tools while I help him. The carving of effigy poles is an old Abenaki tradition, one suppressed by the early Christian missionaries in the Northeast as a work of the devil. Maurice laughs as he tells me that. "It'd be like declaring mailboxes a work of the devil. These poles just say who we are."

Much like the totem poles of the Northwest, each of the effigy poles of the Abenaki tell a story. I know that I have been allowed to watch and help because Mdawelasis wants me to see and feel how this is done, to learn in the old way by both watching and doing. As we work, we hear a sound from overhead, a whistling of wings. We look up and see a loon pass close above us. Mdawelasis means "Little Loon" in Abenaki.

"Heading for Moose River," he says. We watch until it falls out of sight behind the trees. Then he nods and rubs his hand over the shape of Turtle on the half-carved log. "There's thirteen squares on Turtle's shell," he says. "Always thirteen. One for each of the moons. Twenty-eight smaller plates around the outside. One for each of the days in a moon. Always twenty-eight." His hand circles the Turtle's back in a clockwise direction. "Thirteen squares," he says again. "One for each of the Abenaki Nations. Sokoki, Cowasuck, Penacook, Pigwacket. ..." And as he speaks the names of our old nations, I know that I will remember. I, too, will feel the tribes and the seasons beneath my palm as I touch old Turtle's back. Everything in this moment, the smell of wood smoke in the air, the feel of cool earth beneath our bare feet, the sound of his dog Awasos scratching the floor as it stretches on the nearby back porch, will be as clear in my memory as the whistling of the loon's wings which told the old man that the time was right to share this story. So, too, my own mind was open to accept the story. And that was as important, for a story is truly told only when someone listens.

The importance of setting, time and timing in the telling of Native American stories has sometimes been neglected—despite the frequent mentions (to be found in virtually every Native American culture) of the *right time* for stories to be told. However, in books such mentions are usually found in the introductions and, unlike a live storytelling experience, one cannot be sure that those necessary framing words will be noticed. Although American Indian tales have been popular in American "mass culture" for many generations—probably since the first Europeans heard the recounting of a Native American tale translated into a European language—most non-Natives encounter such stories in the pages of a book rather than in the natural setting of the stories, the physical places and seasonal context, which help ensure that the lessons carried by the stories are properly transmitted, that the stories are treated as living things rather than as cultural artifacts or clever bits of artifice. Because there were many hundreds of different Native traditions in pre-Columbian America and because far more of those traditions remain alive than many think, any remarks I make on this subject cannot be seen to be either authoritative or complete. All I can do is point in a certain direction, as did Mdawelasis with a turn of his head, when he directed my eyes to that totem bird flying above us, seen for only a few seconds and then gone. However, there are certain useful generalizations which—after decades of hearing stories from Native tellers and learning to recount them myself—I believe can be made about American Indian storytelling, past and present.

It is important to begin by treating stories with respect. This respect is a respect which acknowledges them as bearers of tradition and representatives of a *particular* Native nation. They are not just "Indian" stories, but beings which are regarded by Native people to be as alive as the breath which carries them from one person to another. Though many stories are found in different forms in diverse Native cultures throughout the continent, it is vitally important to recognize the origin of the tales, to be able to name the Native nation to which a story belongs. Among the Nez Perce, for example, a particular story tells the listener how to choose the right plant—the serviceberry—to make arrows, and how to dry those twigs by the fire. Stories, you see, were meant to instruct. Some of those instructions were general and of a moral nature; others were extremely precise and keyed to the particular material culture. And those teachings, Moral and Practical (as if the two were different), were often linked inextricably together in the tale.

In the 1988 teachers' guide *All My Relations* (published by the Canadian Alliance in Solidarity with Native Peoples), the section on stories and storytelling makes the instructional nature of the traditional tales abundantly clear. As the Ojibway writer Lenore Keeshig-Tobias puts it:

> Storytelling is never done for sheer entertainment; for the stories were and are a record of proud nations confident in their achievements and their way of life. Stories contain information about tribal values, patterns of the environment and growing seasons, ceremonial or religious details, social roles, geographical formations, factual and symbolic data, animal and human traits. [5]

That teaching role of stories is important to remember. Though the plot of a story may be delightful, if the person who retells it is not aware of the message or messages the story is meant to convey, then they may—as far as the story's traditional purpose goes—destroy the story by leaving out things or changing details they think inconsequential. If, in a Penobscot story, mention is made of the two dogs of the culture hero Gluskabe, it is important to know why one of those dogs is black and the other is white. It is because they stand for day and night. Further, those "dogs" are called that in the story, but it is known that they are actually wolves. Mastery over darkness and light and a strong connection with the wild natural world can be seen in the bond between Gluskabe and his dogs when the story is properly told. Retelling the story (as I once heard a non-Indian do it) in a way which describes them as two little dogs, one spotted and the other brown, robs the story of some of its power and turns an important element of the story into nonsense.

The teachings in a great many of the tales are vital ones for all human beings. It was with that in mind that Michael J. Caduto and I created a book called *Keepers of the Earth,* which uses traditional Native stories to teach young people environmental lessons. There is no reason why non-Indians cannot tell Native tales—if they approach them in the right ways. However, a familiarity with the particular Native culture the story comes from and some acquaintance with the living inheritors of that culture is missing among all too many of those who try to tell Indian stories. I will leave this topic for the moment, however, as it is covered in detail in the second part of this essay.

Terry Tafoya is a Skokomish-Pueblo storyteller who has worked extensively as a teacher trainer. In Native cultures, he says, "... education has not been primarily training children to be good hunters or good basket-makers or whatever, but to be good human beings. And that's what stories do." In other words, storytelling teaches proper human values to the young (and old) in a nonauthoritarian way. Tafoya continues:

> With many native people, it's not customary to say "You must not do that." So many of our stories are used to teach about proper behavior, often by teaching what improper behavior is. When you do something against society, you receive all sorts of trials and tribulations. This is to say to children "You may act this way, but look at the consequences." In these stories, the characters are true to their own nature. And that's a purpose of storytelling: teaching people who they are so they can become all they were meant to be.[6]

Timing, as I've said, is important in the telling of a story. In order for a story to really reach the ears of the listeners properly, certain techniques were used, techniques which are common to storytelling practices in other cultures. For one, formulaic phrases which require a response would be spoken to announce the beginning of the storytelling time. Among the Seneca, a storyteller about to recite a *ga-ga'* or folktale would say *"Hanio!"* Only if the response of *"Hah!"* was given could the story then be told. The attention of the listeners had to be focused on the story. If not, it was a waste of the story and the storyteller's effort and the tale would not be continued. Further, the storyteller would continually test the attentiveness of the audience, maintaining their alertness and their involvement. Harriet Maxwell Converse was a white poet who worked closely with the Senecas (and, in particular, Ely S. Parker, the Seneca sachem known as Donehogawa, who was a Civil War Brevet General and personal secretary to Ulysses S. Grant). She spoke of this necessary response to the storyteller in the introduction to her collection of *Myths and Legends of the New York State Iroquois.*

> At intervals during the relation of a story the auditors must exclaim "Hah!" This was the sign that they were listening. If there

was no frequent response of "Hah!" the storyteller would stop and inquire what fault was to be found with him or his story.

It was also considered a breach of courtesy for a listener to fall asleep, but also a positive omen of evil for the guilty party. If any one for any reason wished to sleep or leave the room, he must request the narrator to tie the story, "Si-ga'hah." Failing to say this, and afterwards desiring to hear the remainder of the tale, the narrator would refuse him, for if he related it at all it must be from the beginning through unless tied.[7]

A second characteristic which seems to have been true of traditional Native stories throughout the continent is that certain stories were only to be told at certain times. That time might be during the "storytelling season," during a particular ceremony, at a specific time of day or during a particular activity, or the story might be signaled by an event in the natural world. It may be, for example, that the appearance of the loon told Mdawelasis that it was time to relate certain things to me. In many places in the northeastern part of North America, the time for relating traditional stories is said to be between first frost and last frost. I have also heard it said that the first sound of thunder in the spring means that it is the end of the season for telling stories. In other cases, storytelling had to cease as soon as the seeds were planted. Quoting Lenore Keeshig-Tobias again: "Most traditional stories were told only at night time in the winter. Others were told any time and still others only in ceremonies."[8]

Tehanetorens, a Mohawk elder and storyteller, gave this explanation of the prohibition against telling stories at the wrong time during a talk at his Six Nations Indian Museum in Onchiota, in the Adirondack Mountains of New York:

Over across the ocean, there's a race of people. Those people, especially the Irish, believe there's a little race of people, maybe a foot and a half tall. They call them leprechauns. Now whether or not they existed, I can't say, but many old people think there were little people called leprechauns. Be careful how you treat them. They had great powers. You treat them wrong, they could bring you bad luck. Treat them right, they could bring you good luck.

The old Indians also had a belief in little people. They called them Djogaoh. These Djogaoh made a rule a long time ago. They say these kinds of stories are only to be told in the winter time, when the Mother Earth is asleep. And there's a reason for that. Animals are very psychic. Maybe you didn't know, but animals and birds can understand you, they can read your mind. Maybe an old man's telling a story. Maybe a bird's getting food for her little ones. She flies over that bark house. There's an opening where the smoke comes out. In the summertime there's no smoke, so she listens. She hangs around for maybe half an hour to see how the story comes out. Meanwhile, those little ones are hollering for food, they're going hungry. That bird's not doing her duty.

The Djogaoh made a rule. Don't tell stories in the summertime, because creatures can hear you and they neglect their work. The Djogaoh said that's not right.[9]

Further, the little people are said—in many parts of North America— to enforce that rule. For example, if one of the little people heard someone telling stories at the wrong time, that little person would turn into a bee and sting the person to warn them to stop. The little people, a Seneca storyteller told me in 1988, also do not like to hear stories told about them at the wrong time or in the wrong way. They are jealous of their privacy. One such story of the little ones enforcing their privacy was related to me in 1987 while I was in the mountains of New Hampshire visiting yet another Abenaki elder, Stephen Laurent (Attian Lolo) and his wife, Margie. Among the Abenaki, the little people are called Mannogemassak. They are shy of human contact, though they have been known to give special gifts to those humans who have won their favor. Sometimes, on the riverbanks or buried in deposits of clay, you may be lucky enough to find a specially shaped stone, which looks like an animal perhaps. These are gifts of the little people. As they showed me some of the stones they had, I mentioned finding one myself as I canoed on the Connecticut River. "Then you should hear this story," Margie said. She told me of an Abenaki man, not too many years ago, who wanted to see the little people in the worst way. He was warned not to bother them, but he thought he had a good idea. He would hide under his overturned canoe near the riverbank where they came at night to make their little pots out of clay. When the man did not come back the next day, the people weren't too worried until it got dark again. When he still didn't return on the second morning, they went to look for him. They found his canoe, turned right side up, but there was no sign of the man. Then they saw that there was a long mound of hardened clay by the river, just about the shape of a man with a hole where the mouth would be. They listened at that place and heard breathing and a voice faintly pleading for help. When they broke open the clay, that man who wanted to see the Mang-masak was inside. He never tried that again!

The enforcement of the prohibition against storytelling out of season or disturbing such guardians of the natural order of things as the little people is to be found in many places. In the Southwest, the Pacific Northwest, and the Northeast, it is said that snakes will come into your house if you tell stories at the wrong time. (Although seen as dangerous and deserving of respect, snakes are not viewed by Native Americans in the same way as much of the Western world sees them. In fact, because the snake is so close to the earth, it is often described as a very wise creature, one which knows mysteries that humans do not.) It is also general practice among many Native nations of the far West and Southwest to show particular sensitivity toward Coyote stories in terms of when and how they are told. (Coyote is viewed differently from one tribal nation to the next, though the contemporary "Pan-Indian" view of Coyote in modern American Indian writing is that of a combination hero and buffoon, a trickster in the truest and most complex sense of the word.) For example, certain Navajo friends have told me that Coyote stories are only to be related in a certain setting. Even the mention of the Trickster Coyote's name (especially in a Native language) out of the proper context was regarded as inadvisable. "Say his name," a California Indian storyteller told me, "and he might just decide you want him to come visit you. And you might not like that!"

Clearly, the picture which this gives us of the natural world which surrounded the traditional storytellers and their people was not a world of "dumb" nature. It was an aware and responsive universe. The hunters of the northeastern forest, for example, were extremely careful not to tell during the daytime or the summer months those stories in which animals were tricked by humans. Told at the wrong time, those tales might be overheard by the animals. By hearing such stories, the animals could learn to outwit human hunters or, warned by the tales, simply go away forever from the places humans could find them.

It may also be said that the limiting of the stories to the winter seasons made practical sense in terms of human psychology. Such times were more conducive to attentive listening. The activities of the times of planting and hoeing and harvesting were over, and these times of long nights and short days were the times to draw the people together in the lodges. It should be remembered, of course, that Native people were more active in the outdoors during the wintertime than most present-day Americans—with the exception of those training for the biathlon or cross-country skiing. Certain games, such as the throwing of the long smooth sticks called "snow snakes," could only be done in the season of snows. Snowshoes were a Native invention. (And toboggan, after all, is an Abenaki word.) However, when a winter storm is blowing, when the long night has fallen, one can easily imagine just how much importance a good story told around a warm fire would have.

Storytelling continues to play its traditional roles of entertaining and instructing among the various Native American nations to this day. The TV and the VCR have had their effect among Native Americans, but they have not driven out the practice of storytelling, even though the place where the traditional telling of American Indian tales by Native elders may more often be in a school—such as the En'owkin School of Writing, a Native college in British Columbia or at the Onondaga Nation School, a kindergarten through twelfth-grade school run by the Onondaga Nation near Syracuse, New York—than in a longhouse or council lodge around a fire. Just how important storytelling still is to Native people may not be immediately evident to outsiders—many of whom judge a person as an Indian only if they wear beads and feathers and look like Hollywood's vision of Sitting Bull. In *Spirit of the New England Tribes* (University Press of New England, 1986), William S. Simmons concludes that it is in the continuing folklore of the New England Native peoples that their spirit and their Indian identity have most strongly survived. Their stories have sustained them and kept them alive as a people.

Nosapocket, a Wampanoag storyteller, relates the tale of hearing a sound like heavy footsteps in the woods near Mashpee, Massachusetts. In her story, Nosapocket hides and waits to see what is making the sound.

It turns out to be a tiny green bird, walking in a circle in the clearing. Each time it places a foot on the earth, it sounds like the footsteps of a giant. That story is a very meaningful one for the Wampanoag people. One of the great friends and guardians of the Wampanoag long ago was a giant named Maushop. He brought wood for the people and helped them hunt for food. Finally, though, it was decided that he was spoiling the people too much. The Creator asked him to leave so that the Wampanoag would not become lazy. Sadly, Maushop departed from the lands of his friends. That tiny bird, small as the Wampanoag people and their lands were now small, was the same green color which was associated with Maushop. Though tiny, his footsteps were still those of a giant. Their friend had returned.

▲▼▲

There are a great many contemporary Native American storytellers and virtually all of them have a deep awareness of the importance of their place in preserving values and teachings which are important not just to their Native American nations (though their own tribal nations are the primary ones to whom they wish to tell their stories) but also to all people. Ideas of ecological balance, for example, are stressed repeatedly in Native American tales from all over the continent. It was an easy task for me to put together many such stories for *Keepers of the Earth: Native American Stories and Environmental Activities for Children*.[10]

Both to share such teachings and to make the larger public aware of the proud traditions of their Native nations, more and more American Indian storytellers are putting down their stories in writing. I think this is not, as some would have it, a last-ditch attempt to save dying traditions, but rather an awareness that some of the stories are strong enough to stand on their own, even without the presence of a teller who interprets them through tone, gesture and the contexts of place and time. Lakota storyteller, Moses Big Crow, told me that he published *A Legend from Crazy Horse Clan*[11] because he wanted to share the life of his own ancestors with an unknowing public. He wanted to portray his people not as a "mass of war-loving savages" as in the movies, but as people with intelligence, people who were organized and had principles, people who believed in God and had respect. Because of that decision, he learned to write and prayed to the ancestors for help. The result was a book which I heartily recommend to anyone interested in the lives of the Lakota people or in good storytelling.

This desire to share, even at the risk of sharing with those who may not understand what a powerful gift they have been given, is at the heart of it. More now than ever before, we need the gift of stories which instruct and delight, explain and sustain. Such stories lead us—as that simple tale told me by Mdawelasis on a clear autumn day—to an understanding of who we are and what our place is in the natural world. They help us find respect for ourselves and respect for the earth. They lead us toward understanding the sacred nature of the greatest story of all, that story which is told by the rising sun each dawn, the story of the gift of life.

The Right Time for Stories

While talking with Dovie Thomason, a Lakota storyteller, the topic came up of "when" stories can be told. Like myself, Dovie deals with non-Native tellers who come to her for advice, and when she tells them that certain stories were not traditionally told in the summer, or that there are proper ways to tell certain traditional tales, some people either can't or don't want to understand. "Couldn't I just tell this one story?" people say. Or, "Are you sure about that? I know another Native American who tells stories in the summertime."

Whether people wish to believe in or follow such practices or not, there are a number of formal practices (which vary from nation to nation) connected with traditional Native American storytelling. In many tribal nations, certain stories require a formal invocation. Keewaydinoquay, who is Anishinabe, sings a song before she begins to tell stories and makes an offering of *asseyma* ("Native tobacco") for the ancestors. Those who have studied storytelling with her, Indian and non-Indian alike, do the same. There are also times of the year when stories are to be told—as I mentioned in the first part of this essay. My own experience leads me to believe that it was a continent-wide tradition that the majority of those American Indian traditions called myths and legends by ethnologists were only to be told at certain times of the year. That time was described differently from region to region. In the Northeast it seems to be still classified as the time between first frost and last frost. Many non-Native storytellers bemoan the fact that there is so much call for their Indian stories in the summer—when people have the time to listen—yet that isn't the traditional time to tell them. Children are out of school in the summer and that is about the only time you can get them together around a campfire. I do have some answers for them. In the best of circumstances, the summer is the time when you walk around carrying those stories in your mind and seeing how their lessons apply. The memory and the teachings of those stories are with you, but the natural world is too busy now for you or it to slow down and listen to such stories. Wintertime is for talking the stories, summer is for walking the stories. I also remind people that certain stories may be told in the summer—such things as stories about things that have happened to you and those you know and histories of Native people can sometimes be related in the summertime. I also tell them that though I know some of my stories have been tape recorded and may be played by others in the summertime, they will not hear my living voice telling certain stories except during the moons between first and last frost.

A poet friend of mine wanted to tell Indian tales as I did. However, at the time he neither knew nor cared about prohibitions. He researched some stories from a nineteenth-century text and began to rewrite them in his own words and memorize them. At last he was ready to tell one of them in public. People loved the story, but a strange thing happened. He became very sick after telling the tale. He asked me what I thought about it, and I told him that it might be worth his while to learn more about the stories he was retelling, to find out if there were ways and times they should be told. Instead, he told another of the stories at a public gathering and had a serious accident immediately after leaving the place. Once more, he asked me what I thought. I suggested yet again that he find out more about the stories, that he seek direct information from the Native people whose traditions he was using. Instead, he went to the library and discovered that the stories he was telling were described as stories to be told "only at night during the season when the nights are long." His response was that he now wanted to test this by using the scientific method. He would find out if it was true or not in the only way he could—by telling another of the stories during the day at the wrong time of year. "I don't know if that is a good idea," I wrote back to him. But he wanted to find out if it was just coincidence. He told another of the stories in public at the wrong time. This time he became so ill that he almost died. Not long after, he made a trip to Oklahoma, visited some elders from that Native tribal nation—and ceased telling those stories at the wrong time.

Native American Uses of Stories

Hey-ho-wey—I tell a story,
A story from the Ancient Ones,
Hey-ho-wey—I place asseyma
For their spirits ...
Hey-ho-wey—I tell a story,
Listen and learn.
Hey-ho-wey—Hey-ho-wey ...
—story invocation as sung by
Keewaydinoquay[12]

How are Native American stories used by Indian people? It goes without saying that one important aspect of traditional Native stories is that they are entertaining. The entertainment value of the story is important for at least two reasons. First, of course, because entertainment enlivens the mind and quickens the spirit, especially at those times—in the deep of winter as a storm rages, for example—when nothing other than a story is available to strengthen the hearts of the people. Second, a story must be entertaining so that those who listen to it will focus their full attention. This full attention is needed so that the lesson of the story will go deep into the listener, a lesson which may be almost unnoticed, but is made stronger when the story is truly entrancing.

In every Native American tribal nation, stories have been used since time immemorial to teach the people those lessons they need to cooperate and survive. Native cultures throughout the continent placed high premiums on both the independence of the individual and the importance of working for the good of all. Coercion was seldom used to force the individual to conform, and, to this day, most Native American people hesitate to tell anyone directly—Indian or non-Indian—what they *should* do. Noninterference is a way of life, and people were expected to behave properly because they had been taught the proper ways to behave, not out of fear of legal punishment. The lack of police, strict laws and jails was remarked upon by many European observers of Native communities in the sixteenth, seventeenth and eighteenth centuries, even as they also took note of the fact that there was virtually no crime. The lack of coercion is particularly evident in child-rearing practices. Universally, it was regarded as deeply wrong for adults to beat children. The European rule of "spare the rod and spoil the child" seemed unreasonable and perverse to the Native Americans who saw that beating children generally produces only negative results. It might break a child's spirit or engender deep resentment. Such a cowardly act was also a bad example. Those who beat their children could expect one day to be beaten by those children when they became stronger than their parents. Instead of corporal punishment, the first step taken when a child did wrong was to use the power of storytelling to direct the transgressor in a more positive direction. If a child were, for example, rude to an elder or doing things which endangered the child or others, that child would be told one or more lesson stories designed to show the results of such misbehavior. The power of such stories—which remain in use today in many places—was usually enough. If stories did not work, the next step among the Iroquois was to throw water in the child's face. If that produced no good result, then shunning was the most drastic step taken. The child would be ignored, as if she or he did not exist. Among the Abenaki, the child's face would be blackened and the child would be sent out of the lodge—to be shunned by the whole community. As soon as the child indicated willingness to behave properly, the shunning ceased. (In the case of adults who consistently acted against the welfare of the people or committed some heinous crime—such as murder—the most drastic measure was to banish that person, for a period of a year or for life, from the lands of that tribal nation. Adults, too, might be told stories to help them see the right paths to follow.)

Because lesson stories are of such importance to the welfare of the individual and the nation, they are charged with great power. Not everyone could be entrusted with such power, and to be given permission to tell a certain story meant that you had done the necessary work to become a worthy carrier. Simply having a good memory and being an entertaining actor was not enough. A good story, one which is entertaining and creatively effective in conveying its message, is likely to have an effect upon those who hear it. (This goes back, of course, to the role of the story as a social guide, making it of the utmost importance that the story be memorable.) Because of the power of a story, it is important that a non-Indian who wishes to tell that tale clearly understand the message that particular story is meant to convey. (And some stories have messages at a number of levels, all of which must be understood by the teller.) There must also be a real awareness of the story as something more than just a collection of words or a cultural artifact. A story is a burden which must be carried with as much care as we carry a sleeping child. If a teller is unaware of all the ways in which a particular story might be used, then that teller might be more likely to misunderstand and misuse that tale. Just because it is attractive does not mean that it is right to pick it up. Stories are like food. We eat food because we like its taste and texture, but we also eat it to stay alive. And when traditional Native people eat, giving thanks is as important as the eating itself.

It is no exaggeration to say that all authentic American Indian stories, when used in their proper context, are important tools of communication meant to convey lessons. That remains so true in Native American communities to this day that even joke telling is used in a similar fashion. Vine Deloria Jr., the Lakota Sioux writer, devotes an entire chapter of *Custer Died for Your Sins* to Indian humor. "For centuries," Deloria explains, "before the white invasion, teasing was a method of control of social situations by Indian people."[13] When an Indian tells you a joke, listen closely to it. That joke may be intended as a lesson for you, even an indirect reprimand to let you know that you have overstepped your bounds or given offense in some way. I was once with a group of people who were talking rather insensitively about the problems they'd had working with Indians on a particular reservation. "These people," they said, "just don't know how to be civilized. No wonder the Bureau of Indian Affairs has such problems with them."

A Creek elder who was with me stepped in with this story.

"There was this old Indian man," he said, "standing in front of the BIA building in Washington. Just as this BIA bureaucrat came walking out, that old Indian man had to blow his nose. So he just pinched his nose with his thumb and forefinger and blew his nose onto the grass. Well, that bureaucrat he was disgusted. He thought 'I better show this old man how civilized people should do that.' So he walked right up to that old man. 'Look at this,' the bureaucrat said. Then he reached into his pocket, took out a white handkerchief, shook it out and blew his nose into it, folded it and put it back into his pocket. The old Indian man looked at him for a while and then shook his head. 'Boy, you white people save everything!' the old man said."

There is more to Native American storytelling than just entertaining and conveying lessons. It is not that hard to recognize those two levels of storytelling, but there is also a third level which frequently co-exists with the first two and, in some stories, is of the utmost importance. That is the level of the sacred, of the story as prayer, of storytelling as healing. In contemporary Native American fiction, Leslie Marmon Silko's novel *Ceremony* is a graphic example of the story as sacred healer and spiritual guide. In *Ceremony,* the main character is a young Pueblo man named Tayo who returns from World War II damaged in spirit. It is only through the retelling of the old sacred stories and understanding their meaning in the modern world that he is able to regain his equilibrium.[14] Thinking about this aspect of stories may help those hearing them to begin to perceive the existence of the sacred in stories they already know—or thought they knew. It is important to remember the holistic nature of Native American cultures. There is none of the separation of church and state, none of the convenient pigeonholing which makes it easy for Western political and religious leaders to lead double lives insofar as personal morals go, none of those terms which make it natural to separate the sacred from the everyday. In the universe of American Indian people, everything is sacred.

A book I strongly recommend to anyone interested in the role of stories in contemporary Native American lives is *Wolf That I Am* by Fred McTaggart. It chronicles the efforts in 1971 of McTaggart, then a Ph.D. candidate at the University of Iowa, to collect and write about the stories of the Mesquakie people, whose settlement was not far from Iowa City. Although he thought he would be collecting quaint folktales from the remnants of a dying culture, he soon found himself confronted by people who believed strongly in themselves, their language and their stories.[15] Far from dying, the Mesquakie way was very much alive. Far from being ready to eagerly share their tales with a tape recorder–bearing graduate student, the Mesquakie were politely and firmly protective of their traditions.

At the advice of a Mesquakie friend he called "James Farmer," who was also a student at the university, McTaggart trudged through a snowstorm to reach the house of a man in the Mesquakie community who was said to know many stories. But when McTaggart knocked on Tom Youngman's door and the man stepped out, shutting the door behind him as McTaggart shivered in the cold, this is what happened:

> I was told you might be able to help me out with some information about some stories.
>
> The man's deep brown eyes looked into mine for several minutes. I sensed in his eyes a power and a calmness that I was not at all familiar with. He was wearing only a flannel shirt, but he did not even shiver in the cold piercing wind. As he stood in front of the closed door, looking deeply into my eyes, he somehow put me at ease, and I felt neither the fear nor the guilt that I usually felt when first meeting people on the Mesquakie settlement. His silence was an adequate communication and when he finally spoke, I knew what he was about to say.
>
> "I can't tell you stories," he said softly. I had no trouble hearing him over the whispering wind. "I use my stories to pray. To me, they are sacred."
>
> I thanked him, and he opened his door again and retreated into his small lodge. ...[16]

When McTaggart returned to Iowa City, he realized that he had been tricked by his Mesquakie student friend. At first he was angry and confused, then he realized that by being tricked, as Wolf is tricked by Raccoon in one of the Mesquakie stories he was trying to learn, he had been taught an important lesson.

In many Native American traditions, certain stories are only taught to those who have been properly initiated. In certain cases, stories are an important element in rituals of healing. The most obvious example are the Navajo stories which are part of the healing way ceremonies. Specific figures from a particular story are drawn with colored sand on the earth, and the person seeking to be cured sits in the midst of that sand painting—made a part of the story—in a ceremony which may take a number of days. Entertainment, teaching, healing and prayer—all are aspects of Native American storytelling. There is also another level—that level of obtaining spirit power through the learning of a story. Such power can be used in positive or negative ways. I was told, for example, of a non-Indian writer who spent many years recording the stories from one particular storyteller. He understood that stories were used both to teach and entertain. But one day he was told by certain elders that there was another level—the use of stories in healing. This excited him and he began to look more into the healing level. Then, because of the stories he was asking about storytelling and power, someone suggested he should visit a certain man. He visited that man and they talked about stories and power late into the night. Then the man said to him, "Who is it that you wish to have die?" The writer was shocked and didn't understand. "From the questions you have been asking me," the old man said to him, "it seems that you wish that kind of power." That power to destroy was connected to those stories, stories which were not just about life and death.

What is the path which should be taken by the non-Indian storyteller when she or he discovers a story that they wish to tell is a story which has qualities of healing or special power? Can that storyteller go ahead and tell the tale outside of its true context without producing some sort of negative effect? Perhaps the best guidance can be found in the stories themselves. You find plenty of examples there of characters who take the sacred too lightly. With the stories, at least, they always pay for their mistakes. Although I cannot tell others what they should or should not do, I do know that taking sacred things lightly is never wise. Perhaps the best advice is that caution is better than foolhardiness and that patience is an underestimated virtue.

Native American Stories and Non-Native Tellers: Some Problems

There is a great deal of interest in Native American tales throughout storytelling circles in America. Almost every storyteller seems to know and tell at least one such story. These "Indian legends" are often among their favorites and the storytellers also find that their audiences ask for and respond to those tales with enthusiasm.

On one level, it is understandable that there should be this interest in Native stories here; after all, this country was founded on "Indian Land." And it was, it seems, founded on certain Native American cultural practices and principles as well. Americans today live more like the Native people they first encountered on this continent than they do like their own European ancestors. In terms of material culture, Americans are much more Indian than they realize. The long list of food plants alone, from corn, beans, squash and potatoes to cocoa and chocolate, has been recited many times over in such volumes as Jack Weatherford's *Indian Givers,* published in 1988, which points out that 60 percent of the food eaten in the world today is of Native American origin.[17] Our American forms of government may owe a stronger debt to the League of the Iroquois, which provided Franklin and Washington with the example which would evolve into the Constitution, than to any European models.[18] The ideas of the relative equality of women (an idea still not fully achieved in Western culture as of today), of leaders ruling with the consent of the governed and of people choosing their own leaders are ideas that were totally foreign to the Europe of the monarchs so firmly in place in 1492. However, the depth of connection to Native antecedent is neither consciously recognized nor acknowledged by Western culture, although the romantic fascination with things "Indian" may be in part a subconscious recognition of those ties.

It is, of course, also true that the stories of the many Native nations of the Western Hemisphere speak to both the Indian and the non-Indian American in ways which no other tales can. It was, of course, Michael Caduto's and my own long recognition of the clear ecological teachings in a great many such stories which led us to produce *Keepers of the Earth.* Moreover, there are so *many* stories. The Native American oral traditions which have been collected, translated into English and published constitute one of the richest bodies of "myth and legend" to be found anywhere in the world. Tens of thousands of Native tales from the more than four hundred different oral traditions of North America can be found in the books of our libraries. To obtain an idea of how extensive these bodies of literature are, one need only look at a 1969 publication by Paul Weinman, *A Bibliography of the Iroquoian Literature,* a book which has long since been far outdated. In the section on "Folklore and Mythology," he lists more than thirty book-length collections of such stories from Iroquois traditions.[19] The attractions of Iroquois tales, stories filled with such exciting details—for both storytellers and audiences—as stone giants, flying heads, vampire skeletons, monster bears and magical little people, can easily be understood. And this from only one Native group of the hundreds to be found, each with their own rich traditions.

It is not surprising, then, that many storytellers view American Indian tales as untapped and fertile ground—virgin land. (Where did we hear that phrase before?) A non-Indian storyteller first "discovering" an American Indian tale which speaks to her or him in a special way must feel as Balboa (not Cortés, Mr. Keats) felt on that peak in Darien when he first saw the Pacific Ocean, overlooking the Native people already living there. But America's "virgin land," as more accurate contemporary histories are now acknowledging, was not a neglected wilderness, but an intimately known and well-cared-for land which was—as in the case of the Pilgrims who were allowed by the Wampanoags to use land recently vacated because of the devastations of a wave of Western-introduced diseases just before those Brits landed not on but some miles down the beach from Plymouth Rock (yes, another myth)—not virgin, but widowed. And, so too, Native stories are not abandoned children waiting to be adopted but living relatives still connected to Earth and people in ways which are not always easy to see at first glance.

There are, you see, a number of problems related to the current uses and misuses of American Indian traditional stories by non-Indian tellers. Even those ethnologists who have lived long and studied deeply just one particular Native nation's traditions have often found themselves making mistakes or failing to see the real point of what they've been seeing until after years of intimate contact, so it ought not to be surprising that those who just "pick up" a story that they think is lying around unused (such as, let's say, a band of outer space aliens wandering around a sleeping city at night, picking up parked cars and plucking stoplights from their posts because those things have obviously been abandoned without ownership) can easily err in recognizing just what it is that they have found, how it is to be properly used and to whom it truly belongs.

That very newness which makes Native American tales so attractive, the "exotic" nature of the stories (strangers now in their own native lands), points to the root of the problem. In large part, even after hundreds of years of "coming to America" (quoting either Neil Diamond, Eddie Murphy or Art Buchwald), non-Natives do not know where they are. They remain blind to the land and to the real (not stereotyped) aspects of Native American cultures, past and present. The very fact that most contemporary non-Native storytellers still find the Indian "myths and legends" that they tell in a book, rather than from the lips of an American Indian, is symptomatic. Often those written versions, some of them out-and-out fakes, others poorly rendered, are accepted as absolutely authentic. Yet any real student of Native cultures (much less a Native person herself or himself) knows that all too many of the written versions of Native American stories are incompletely or inaccurately recorded.

It is a sad truth that the average non-Indian American, today, knows much less about real Native Americans than did the first European settlers on this continent—who survived only because of the active help and gracious friendship of Native Americans. Even those who live within a few miles of large and active contemporary American Indian communities either know little about their Indian neighbors or express the opinion that "there are no more Indians around here." Again and again, I have been in a town and on asking where the local Indians were I've been told "there ain't none," only to meet several local Indians immediately thereafter. American myths—such as the one of the "Vanishing Red Man"—are more alive in the public mind than the presence of Native people, who make up a vital, continent-wide, growing population. If you keep your eyes open, "You meet Indians everywhere," as Simon Ortiz, a Pueblo storyteller and poet, says in his poem "I Told You I Like Indians."[20]

As one might expect, along with that general ignorance of the existence of present-day Native Americans outside of Hollywood movie lots goes a lack of awareness of the place and proper uses of American Indian stories. They are not "myths and legends," in the popular sense, stories which are untrue and belong to some distant past. They are, in fact, alive. No story (as many fine professional storytellers *do* understand) exists in isolation. Stories are a part of the life of the people. The problems of the rationale for effectively and validly transplanting stories from one culture to another do not just relate to American Indian tales. The best contemporary storytellers are usually aware of such problems and engage in heroic efforts to understand the origins and cultural contexts of the tales they use. Some storytellers even refuse to tell any stories outside of their own cultural frames of reference. By and large, I am convinced of the positive, vital role which the resurgence of storytelling is playing in the United States and throughout the world. It is a movement concerned with issues of morality and human interrelationships which go far beyond the mere telling of interesting tales. Quite frankly, if I were not convinced of the good intentions and continued growth of the contemporary community of non-Indian storytellers, I doubt that I would be spending the time to write this essay. Yet many contemporary storytellers know only that the American Indian "myths" they have learned and tell publicly come from this or that book collected, translated or retold by a non-Indian. Ironically, they may know less about the origin of an American Indian story—that grew from this soil—than they do about one from ancient Babylon. Almost universally, non-Native tellers have never heard a word spoken in the particular language from which their Native American tale came, have little knowledge of the intellectual or material cultures of that particular Native people and have never met a living American Indian from that tribal nation. As I've indicated earlier, they may not even know where the story comes from in precise terms, just that it is generic "Indian." In such an atmosphere, it is virtually certain that these tellers do not understand why Native people may object to their telling certain stories, an atmosphere of ignorance in which non-Native tellers know nothing of the strong relationship which exists between storytelling and the sacred throughout the many Native American nations.

Let me make it quite clear, once again, that my aim is not to discourage non-Indians from telling Native American stories. Many of the stories of Native American people have become, to a degree, a visible and even vital part of the heritage of all Americans. This is especially true of certain of the lesson stories, which have never been more needed by human beings than they are now. Many of these stories, which teach people—in a clear and memorable way—the understanding needed to live in ecological and social balance on this planet with all our relations, are stories which are gifts for all human beings. These stories, like the great epic of the founding of the Iroquois League of Peace, are as powerful as medicine and the healing they provide is needed. But, like medicine, like the tobacco which can be used to carry prayers to the Creator, these stories, too, must be used wisely and well or they may bring harm to teller and listener alike. And there are other stories which would be best left alone by non-Native tellers.

Over the last decade I have spoken to many Native American storytellers about the use of their stories by non-Native people. Jeanette Armstrong in British Columbia, Gayle Ross in Texas, Ignacia Broker in Minnesota, Ed Edmo in Oregon, Keewaydinoquay in Michigan, Harold Littlebird in New Mexico, Kevin Locke in North Dakota, Tehanetorens in New York and numerous others have voiced their concern about the use—without permission and with inadequate preparation—of stories from their traditions by non-Native tellers. Yet all of them agree that there is no reason why non-Native tellers who understand and show the proper respect should not tell certain Native American stories. They also know, as do I, that some people will go ahead and do something even if (or perhaps even *because*) they are told *not* to do it. I live only a few miles away from a body of water which was regarded as very special by the Iroquois and Abenaki people, Saratoga Lake. It was known to them that the spirit of the lake demanded respect and that when crossing its waters to the opposite shore, one had to remain silent. If anyone spoke loudly, their canoe would sink. This story was well known to the non-Natives who came to live in nearby settlements and, in general, they respected that tradition, especially when they were being ferried from one shore to the other by the Native boatmen. One day, a woman who was a great skeptic and regarded all Indian beliefs as foolish superstition resolved she would prove this belief to be untrue. She hired a boat with two Indian paddlers, waited until they were in the exact middle of the lake and then shrieked at the top of her lungs. Nothing happened. The boat did not sink. Even the two Indian paddlers seemed to pay no heed to her shout, and she sat there as they finished their trip across, certain that she had proven her point and that the two who had ferried her across now recognized their belief to be false. But as soon as they reached the other side and stepped onto shore, the two Indians turned to each other and nodded. "The spirit of the lake is very understanding," one of them said. "It knows that white people just can't keep their mouths shut." (There is a point, of course, when tolerance is exhausted. At that point, it is said, the stories which do not wish to be told will turn back on those who tell them.)

It is my hope and, I believe, the hope of a number of other Native American storytellers, that by good example and patient explanation, they may help those who are not Native Americans but have a sincere wish to do a good job of telling Native American tales. My words are one attempt to help point such people in directions they might follow to find relationship with those stories.

Native American Stories and Non-Native Tellers: Some Suggestions

What I'd like to share, here, is not a set of hard and fast rules, but some directions a non-Indian storyteller might follow when she or he wishes to use Native American tales. They come from my own approach to the stories I tell, ones which come from the traditions of my own Abenaki ancestors and other Native people from whom I have learned. To begin with, let me explain my own approach to learning and telling stories, one which combines both oral transmission and literary research.

I know a great many stories and each time I travel, I learn more. Some of those stories are what can be called traditional, stories which come from long ago and have been passed down from generation to generation. (All of my following remarks have to do with this one class of story—not stories of personal experience, things which happened to actual people I know, stories which have been given to me directly by the natural world or in dreams.) When I am told such traditional stories and I wish to retell them myself, I always ask the one who told me the story if I can have permission to tell that tale. If they agree, I tell them how I have heard it, making sure that I know the story well enough to tell correctly. I've been blessed with a very good memory and the ability to express things well. Many years ago I was given an Iroquois name by Dewasentah, one of the Clan Mothers at Onondaga because, as she put it, "You've been given a special gift by the Creator and you need an Iroquois name." She had written the name down on an envelope, which contained a small eagle feather and a miniature lacrosse stick. That name, *Gah ne goh he yoh,* which means the "Good Mind," not only gives me strength, it also reminds me of the responsibility I must carry.

I should add, at this point, that just because I have learned a story and been given permission to tell it does not mean that I will actually tell that story. For every story I know and tell, there are many others I know and do not tell. In some cases it is because I feel I do not yet know enough about the story. I have to live with it longer. Further, I like to concentrate on telling those stories which come from the part of the continent I know best—the northeastern woodlands and the traditions of Abenaki and Haudenosaunee (Iroquois). Perhaps the time may not seem right to tell those other stories, perhaps they are stories I will never tell except to other Native people, perhaps the knowing of some of those stories is enough. I *never* tell a story if I have been told that I do not have permission to tell it. Further, permission to tell a story is not the same as permission to publish it in print, to record it or to rewrite it. Retelling a story in your own words is a risky thing because you may lose the heart or obscure the meaning. In certain types of stories, there are always differences in delivery and even in some of the actual words used from one storyteller to another, but the stories are recognizably the same story. Putting a story in print means exposing it to a much larger audience as does doing a voice recording.

At this point, I should introduce the second half of my technique in learning and preparing to tell traditional stories. After hearing a story, I always research thoroughly the written versions which have been recorded in the past. In some cases, say the Abenaki story of "The Wind Eagle," there may be many other versions written down, some of them in both the Abenaki original and a line-by-line English translation. Some Haudenosaunee stories, for example the tale of "How Turtle Made War on Human Beings," may exist in as many as a dozen different versions. Further, that particular story can be found in other Native nations, too. I familiarize myself with the written versions as well as the oral version I have been told. It is *only* when there is already a written version of a story that I will then write down my own version of a story. I have no wish to be the first to publish a traditional tale, and I always try to publish what I feel to be a better and truer version than those which are already in print. Since the story has already been exposed to print, I do not feel that I am breaking the link of oral tradition or betraying something by doing this. If anything, as years go by and I learn more stories and learn more about the stories I already know, I am more rather than less careful about the traditional stories which I record on tape or put into a book. This does not mean that I avoid making mistakes entirely, but it does mean that the mistakes I make tend to be smaller ones. And I always listen to criticism and try to accept it in a humble way. The Haudenosaunee say that a leader must have a skin which is seven thumbs thick and that is true for anyone who deliberately puts themselves into the public eye. In 1989, for example, a Seneca storyteller cautioned me about telling certain stories about the little people. They don't like to hear those stories told about them, she explained. I have heeded her words of caution and no longer tell one particular story. There is always more to learn, and no one ever learns it all. But, if we are both humble and patient, we may learn enough.

▲▼▲

Here are some suggestions:

1. Instead of taking Native American tales solely from books, learn them from the Native storytellers themselves and from the lives of Native people. Visit Native American people to find out more about their ways of life and the way they speak. A very easy way to make contact with Indian people in a nonintrusive fashion is to go to a powwow. Powwows are festivals which are open to the public and are held from spring through late fall. Native people love to have non-Indians at most powwows because it is a time when Native people display and sell all kinds of craftwork, have dance contests, drum and sing and meet old and new friends. Many people, Native and non-Native alike, end up developing lifelong friendships as a result of going to powwows.

I mention the powwow as a nonintrusive means of meeting Native people because it is important to recognize that when you visit Indian land—go to a reservation, for example—you are a visitor and a guest. Keep your eyes and ears open and *don't* ask too many questions. Be polite and patient and accept whatever you are given. Don't walk into people's homes uninvited. If there is a museum or a cultural center open to the public, go there. Tehanetorens's Six Nations Indian Museum in Onchiota, New York (near Saranac Lake in the Adirondacks), has been a place where I have learned much more about storytelling and Native life than from any books.

When visiting Native people, remember that listening and patience are cardinal virtues. The old stereotype of the stoic, silent Indian comes in part from the fact that non-Indians tend to monopolize conversations and ask rhetorical questions. It is common practice in American culture to interrupt others in midsentence when engaged in conversation. Such interruptions effectively terminate all conversation with Native Americans. If you do ask questions, wait for the answers! Avoid leading questions or ones with a simple "yes" or "no" answer. (Remember that "yes" is more polite than "no," and often Native American people may simply say "yes" to agree with you.)

2. When you make use of written texts, fully research the story before you go any further. Some written texts are out-and-out fakes, phony Indian stories. (Many of which tell of the tragic romance between an "Indian Maid" and her lover who is from "another tribe," who both end up jumping off a cliff or going over Niagara Falls or whatever. ...) If you can find a text in the original language with a line-by-line translation, study it carefully. A knowledge of the language and the people from whom the story comes is essential. This includes a real knowledge of the material culture of that tribal nation. It will help you develop a relationship to the story which is vital. It is hard to tell someone, today, how to drive a car unless one knows how to drive, but non-Native storytellers continually tell Native American tales which make reference to aspects of Indian material culture that they have never seen, felt or understood. If you are going to tell a story about a basket, learn how to *make* that basket first.

3. Know what type of story it is that you are learning. Is it a story which is appropriate for you to tell? What does the story teach? What are the levels of teaching in the story? Find out if there are certain times or places when this story is supposed to be told—or not supposed to be told. Be aware of how the story's construction fits into the culture and worldview of that particular Native nation. If you are not certain of a story's meaning or origin, *don't tell it!* If you wish to use a story which you have heard from a particular Native American teller, *always get that person's explicit permission* to tell it. If that person says "no," do not argue with them, just accept it and don't tell that story.

4. When telling Native American stories, avoid racist language or language which stereotypes. Native people find it very insulting when a woman is referred to as a "squaw," a child as a "papoose" and a young man as a "brave." (It is similar to referring to a black child as a "pickaninny" and a young black man as a "buck," language which dehumanizes.) Racist images and racist language have disappeared to some extent from mass and popular culture for every ethnic group in America but one—the Native Americans. In 1995, just before a major league baseball game, a group of fans painted a pig red, tied a feathered headdress on it and chased it across the field. Many people thought it was funny or harmless. Yet how would they have reacted if that poor animal had been painted black with an Afro wig? Think of the tremendous irony of the still widely used term "Indian giver" when you consider the generosity with which the Native people of New England treated the pilgrims.

Remember that Native Americans were often politically and culturally more sophisticated than the early Europeans who encountered them. Those first European colonists described the Indians as tall, healthy, handsome, open, friendly and generous. They lived longer than the Europeans (until the introduction of European plagues), chose their own leaders, enjoyed relative equality of the sexes and made work seem like play. The English colonists envied, emulated and even, in many cases, joined them. The laws against men wearing long hair in Massachusetts (laws still on the books) were designed to keep white men from looking like and becoming Indians. To quote Alvin Josephy, "Belief in the freedom and dignity of the individual was deeply ingrained in many Indian societies."[21] Josephy's *The Indian Heritage of America* is a book that non-Native tellers of Indian stories ought to read.

▲▼▲

One of my favorite stories from Haudenosaunee traditions, which I've mentioned in an earlier essay, is the tale of the Storytelling Stone. It relates how the first stories were taught to a boy by an ancient rock. In exchange for each story he was told, the boy gave the great stone a present. It is an important tale for all of us who wish to share Native American traditions with the world, for it reminds us of the principles of reciprocity and right relation to Earth which are at the heart of Native American stories and culture. Storytellers who keep those principles in mind will be well on their way to using American Indian stories as they were meant to be used—for all our relations, for the people, for Earth.

Notes

1. E. A. Smith, *Myths of the Iroquois* (Washington, DC: U.S. Bureau of American Ethnology, 2nd Annual Report, 1880–81, 1883).
2. Ella E. Clark, *Indian Legends from the Northern Rockies* (Norman: University of Oklahoma, 1966).
3. The Nez Perce Tribe of Idaho, *Nu Mee Poom Tit Wah Tit (Nez Perce Legends)* (n.p: n.p. 1972).
4. Arthur C. Parker, *Seneca Myths and Folk Tales* (Buffalo: Buffalo Historical Society, 1923).
5. Catharine Verrall, comp., *All My Relations: Sharing Native Values through the Arts* (Toronto, Canada: Canadian Alliance in Solidarity with Native Peoples, 1988).
6. Ibid.
7. Harriet Maxwell Converse, *Myths and Legends of the New York State Iroquois* (New York: New York State Museum Bulletin 125, 1908).
8. Catharine Verrall, comp., *All My Relations: Sharing Native Values through the Arts* (Toronto, Canada: Canadian Alliance in Solidarity with Native Peoples, 1988).
9. Ray Fadden (Tehanetorens), *The Gift of the Great Spirit* (Greenfiled Center, NY: Good Mind Records, 1988), audiocassette.
10. Michael J. Caduto and Joseph Bruchac, *Keepers of the Earth: Native American Stories and Environmental Activities for Children* (Golden, CO: Fulcrum Publishing, 1988).
11. Moses Nelson Big Crow, *A Legend from Crazy Horse Clan* (Chamberlain, SD: Tipi Press, 1987).
12. Keewaydinoquay, *MukwahMiskomin: Gift of Bear* (n.p.: Miniss Kitigan Drum, 1977).
13. Vine Deloria Jr., *Custer Died for Your Sins* (New York: Avon Books, 1970).
14. Leslie Marmon Silko, *Ceremony* (New York: Viking Press, 1977).
15. For two very different views of the Mesquakie people, compare the non-Indian poet W. D. Snodgrass's response to visiting a Mesquakie festival in his poem *Pow-Wow* (in *After Experience* [New York: Harper and Row, 1958]), which equates contemporary Native Americans with bugs smashed on the windows of cars, and Mesquakie poet Ray Young Bear's response to that very poem in his *For the Rain in March: The Blackened Hearts of Herons* (in *Winter of the Salamander* [San Francisco: Harper and Row, 1980]).
16. Fred McTaggart, *Wolf That I Am* (Boston: Houghton Mifflin, 1976).
17. Jack Weatherford, *Indian Givers* (New York: Crown Publishing, 1988).
18. José Barriero, ed., "Indian Roots of American Democracy," *Northeast Indian Quarterly* (Ithaca, NY: American Indian Program, Cornell University, 1988).
19. Paul Weinman, *A Bibliography of the Iroquoian Literature* (New York: New York State Museum, Bulletin # 411, 1969).
20. Simon Ortiz, *Woven Stone* (Tucson: University of Arizona Press, 1992).
21. Alvin M. Josephy, *The Indian Heritage of America* (New York: Alfred A. Knopf, 1968).

Digging into Your Heart

Hidden Treasure in Native American Stories

✦

Gladys Tantaquidgeon, a Mohegan elder and cofounder of the Mohegan Indian Museum in Uncasville, Connecticut, told me this story.

Sometime around 1900, Burrill Fielding, the uncle of Gladys Tantaquidgeon, had the same dream three nights in a row—a sure sign that the dream was going to come true. In it, he found himself walking at midnight in the old Shantup burying ground near the river. Each time he came to a stand of three white birches near a flat rock. That was the place to dig. Finally, after the third time he had that dream, he asked Henry Dolbeare, another Mohegan, to go with him that night to the spot he had seen. They took their shovels with them and, sure enough, they found that spot. It was close to midnight, and they started to dig, neither one of them saying a word. To speak when you were digging for a pirate's treasure would make that treasure go away. The bright light of a full moon shone down on them as they dug, and soon Burrill Fielding's shovel struck something that sounded wooden and hollow. Just at that moment, a big black animal jumped down into the hole between them. Both men let out a yell, dropped their shovels and ran away as fast as they could. When Burrill Fielding finally got up the courage to come back to get the shovels—several days later in the middle of the day—he found the shovels resting on that rock, and the hole they had dug was filled in.

"Uncle Burrill," Gladys Tantaquidgeon said, "never went digging at midnight again!"

▲▼▲

There are, of course, many elements in that story which appear to come directly from Western folklore. The themes of buried treasures and murdered men whose ghosts become supernatural guardians are familiar ones in both European American and European traditions. As William S. Simmons points out in *Spirit of the New England Tribes: Indian History and Folklore, 1620–1984*:

The treasure story is a category of folk narrative that is widespread and particularly well represented in historic American, West European, Caribbean and Latin American oral traditions. The stories are not indigenous to the New England Indians, and none were recorded among them until the twentieth century. ...

The Euro-American treasure legend usually involves pirates who bury their ill-gotten wealth and kill one of their crew, whose ghost guards the chest or kettle filled with gold.[1]

The coast of Connecticut where the Mohegan people live was a familiar place for such notorious pirates as Captain Kidd, and many sites, including one particular area up the Thames River close to the present-day Mohegan community, have been said to be places where he buried his treasure. For centuries now people have looked for that treasure. Poe's famous story, "The Gold Bug," is one of the best-known literary treatments of that theme and takes place in roughly the same landscape.

But the Mohegan story of Captain Kidd's treasure, though it may seem familiar, has a different slant. The point of Poe's tale is the figuring out of a mystery. Wealth comes to the treasure seekers as a result of their intellectual puzzle solving—and their defiling of a pirate grave. In the Mohegan tale, the knowledge of the treasure's location is arrived at through purely supernatural means—by way of a dream vision. And just when the two Mohegan men are about to uncover the treasure, it is taken away from them under equally mystical circumstances.

The messages held in a story of seeking pirate treasure may, it appears, be quite different when the tale is told as part of the traditions of a Native American people, even when that story is told in a way which seems completely in line with European-American traditions. It is not just the *how* of the story's telling, it is also the *why*. To better understand what those messages might be, one needs to look at other, older Native tales which deal with that related theme of finding your heart's desire.

▲▼▲

One such story is found widely among the Wabanaki peoples farther up along the New England coast. Over the years I have found versions of this tale among the Micmac, the Penobscot and my own Western Abenaki people. It tells how four men make a difficult journey to visit Gluskabe, the powerful ancient being who did many things to make the earth a better place for his human "grandchildren" before retiring to an island shrouded in a magical mist created by the tobacco smoke from his pipe.

Each of the men has a wish, and Gluskabe grants those wishes. Each is given a pouch and told not to open it until they are within their own lodges. Three of those wishes, however, are selfish ones and the fulfilling of those wishes brings ironic consequences. Not only that, the first three men are so eager to get their heart's desire that they each open their pouches before they reach their homes. The man who wishes to be taller than all others becomes a tree. The one who wishes never to die becomes a stone. The one who wishes to have more possessions than anyone else is given so many things that it sinks his canoe and he is drowned, covered by his possessions. Only the fourth man, whose wish is to be able to better help his people, waits until he is in his lodge before opening his pouch. He finds that the pouch is empty, but when he opens it, good thoughts come into his mind and he finds within his own heart that which was formerly hidden from him. In one version of the story it is the knowledge needed to be a better hunter, in another it is the knowledge needed to show his people the right ways to live.

▲▼▲

There are few stories which do a better job of pointing out the difference between Native American and European attitudes about treasure than do these two tales. Even when the worlds of European attitudes and Native traditions come into direct and jarring conflict—in an Indian burial ground where pirate wealth is hidden in a grave—the values which are upheld and strengthened in these tales are ones which are very old and very much American Indian. But what are those "Native" values and what are the lessons conveyed by these stories?

The lessons are easier to find in the story of the four wishes. One lesson is about the danger of self-centered wishes and actions. To desire things which benefit only yourself will eventually result in your own downfall. To wish something which will bring good to your people will produce good results for everyone. Handsome Lake, the Seneca prophet, was visited by Four Messengers while he lay in an alcoholic coma in June 1800, a time when his people had lost most of their land and were deep in despair, on the verge of losing everything else. He was given a vision intended to help guide him and his people back from the brink of destruction. As they took him along the sky road of the Milky Way, pointing out the evils which his people must avoid, one of the things he was shown illustrated the results of such wrong desires:

> Now they said to him
> "We will pause here
> in order for you to see."
>
> And as he watched,
> he saw a large woman
> sitting there.
> She was grasping frantically
> at all the things
> within her reach
> and because of her great size
> she could not stand.
> That was what he saw.
>
> Then they asked him,
> "What did you see?"
>
> He answered,
> "It is hard to say.
> I saw a woman of great size,
> snatching at all that was about her.
> It seemed she could not rise."
> Then the messengers answered,
> "It is true.
> What you saw was the evil of greed,
> She cannot stand
> and will remain thus forever.
>
> Thus it will always be with those
> who think more of the things of earth
> than of this new world above.
> They cannot stand upon the heaven road."

There is a second message, too, to be found within the story of the four wishes. The man who waits, showing the virtue of patience and the necessity of following the instructions of elders, is given what he desires. But it is not anything material. Instead it is knowledge, found, it is sometimes said, by looking into his heart. There is a word in the Cree language which describes the place that knowledge and stories come from. It is, it seems, the center of creativity. That word is *achimoona* and it translates as the "sacred place within." The Micmac people speak of the "great man inside," a spiritual being which is held within each person's heart and who will provide good guidance if heeded. The Lakota tell the story of the Seventh Direction, the last direction to be placed by Wakan Tanka and the most powerful of all. But because Wakan Tanka feared that the human beings would misuse that power if it was too easy to find, it was hidden in the last place most people think to look—inside each person's heart. Although there are other lessons which can be drawn from that story of the four wishes, I believe that the greatest one is that we will only find peace and fulfillment when we are able to look into our own hearts while thinking of the common good. Although more than four hundred different Native cultures and languages are found within the North American continent and there are great differences between those cultures and languages, the lessons of that Wabanaki story seem to hold true for all Native traditions. Father Claude Chauchetiere, who was a priest at the Mohawk mission of Kahnawake (near present-day Montreal), wrote the following (which was collected in the *Jesuit Relations* and later published in 1981 in the *Narrative of the Mission of Sault St. Louis, 1667–1685*):

> We see in these savages the fine roots of human nature which are entirely corrupted in civilized nations. ... Living in common, without disputes, content with little, guiltless of avarice ... [2]

The context which this interpretation of the Wabanaki story of the four wishes creates helps us see into the heart of Gladys Tantaquidgeon's tale of frustrated treasure seekers. It is, by the way, a story which is also found in varying forms among other peoples of that southern New England coast, including the Pequots and the Wampanoags. A Wampanoag tale written down in 1934 by Mrs. Frederick Gardner, herself a Mashpee

Wampanoag, tells the story of Hannah Screecham, a Wampanoag woman who befriended the pirates and helped them in the burial of their treasure and the accompanying murder of the sailors who would guard those gold-filled graves. But when Hannah went to dig up some of that treasure for herself, she was strangled by the ghosts of those murdered men.

Bearing in mind the lessons taught by the story of the four wishes, one easily discerned message in this story and other Native New England tales of such failed quests for buried treasure is that a desire for personal, selfish gain dooms the seeker to, at best, failure and, at worst, destruction. But there is another message which is held, I am certain, in these stories. It is so much a part of the consciousness of all Native peoples of North and South America that we sometimes forget that European Americans do not share or understand this point of view, this feeling which Native peoples have about "buried treasure," about gold and graves.

In contrast to the tradition in pirate legends of burying someone else with your gold—gold which you plan to dig up and use at a later time (the eighteenth-century equivalent of an IRA?)—the Native traditions of the Americas frequently included interring material possessions as "grave goods" to go in spirit with the deceased person into the next life. The idea of digging up those grave goods, whether they were gold ornaments to wear or baskets filled with corn to feed the spirit, was an abomination. Yet the digging up of such graves by professional archaeologists, "pot hunters" and fortune seekers continues to this day. Wampanoag traditions indicate that when the ill-prepared Pilgrims of the Plymouth Colony arrived in Massachusetts, the Native people watched them for some time before deciding whether or not to approach them. Although Squanto (who was clearly a man of a forgiving nature, having just made his way back to Massachusetts after being taken some years before to Europe as a slave by another group of Englishmen) finally made the fateful decision to assist them, many of the Wampanoags urged him not to do so. They had observed the Pilgrims digging up Indian graves to obtain the baskets of corn buried there as food for the dead, something even a starving Native would never have done.

Throughout the Americas, there are still stories told of lost Indian gold, from the Seven Cities of Cibola in the American Southwest to the South American tale of El Dorado, the lake where a fabled "chief" would coat his body with gold and then wash it off in the waters as a sacrifice. Even the Adirondack Mountains of New York State have one such story. It is said (in a story which seems to have originated with Jed Rossman, a tall tale teller who worked for years at Adirondack Loj in the heart of the High Peaks) that there is a hidden cave filled with Indian treasure on the side of Mount Colden. That cave can only be seen when standing on another nearby peak at midnight on a full moon in the month of August. But the treasure in that cave, which was brought there by Kahnawake Mohawk and St. Francis Abenaki Indians on their way back north after a raid in 1690 on Schenectady, is guarded by the ghost of a giant Indian.

Whether such stories hold a grain of truth or not, they are part of the popular mind-set about "Indian treasures." It does not matter if those treasures are grave goods or sacrifices to the spirits. Quite simply, that hidden wealth, placed by Native people to rest forever in the breast of the earth, is there for the taking. And, until quite recently, all of the archaeological community felt the same about the wealth of knowledge to be discovered in Native graves. It was there for the taking. Although it has long been illegal to dig up the graves of non-Natives, finding and exhuming Native remains was standard practice throughout the last four centuries and, in a number of American states, it is still perfectly legal. The repatriation to Native peoples of the remains of their ancestors who were dug up by "scientific researchers" is a very new phenomena. Some Native communities, like my own Abenaki people, believe that bad luck has come to both the white and Indian communities alike as a result of those ancestors not being placed back to rest. Yet even those enlightened non-Native people who have agreed to return human remains still find it hard to understand that the "grave goods" are also supposed to be returned so that the journey to the spirit world can be continued in the proper way. I recall a meeting in the 1980s (which the Abenaki Nation has on videotape) in which several hours were spent trying to explain that point to a group of archaeologists who didn't understand why the return of the bones was not enough. Thus, we may also hear Gladys Tantaquidgeon's story of the failed treasure hunt— and such legends as that of Hannah Screecham—as teaching tales and a response to that long-standing European passion for grave robbing. The dead, and whatever has been sent with them to the next world, must be left in peace. Those who do not heed that injunction will find themselves confronted by guardians from the spirit world. No one, whether Indian or non-Indian, should disturb Indian graves, and Native people should not fall into the trap of the avaricious thinking which seems to characterize much of European culture.

The 1990s have brought a further irony to the locale of that first story I told. Where European Americans once sought out Captain Kidd's buried millions, crowds now flock to Indian-run casinos in the state of Connecticut. Because of current federal laws which recognize the special "sovereign" status of Native lands, gambling operations are legal on Indian reservations and hundreds of casinos have been constructed and are bringing new wealth to Native communities—among them are the Mashuntucket Pequots and the Mohegans. With that new wealth—and all of the dangers of corruption brought by such sudden riches—flowing into those previously impoverished Native communities, such stories as the tale of the four wishes and the search for pirate treasure may take on a new meaning for Native communities. Understanding that meaning may help them make the right wishes, help them remember that the only place to dig for the true treasure is in your heart.

Notes

1. William S. Simmons, *Spirit of the New England Tribes: Indian History and Folklore, 1620–1984* (Hanover, NH: University of New England, 1986).
2. Reuben Gold Thwaites, *The Jesuit Relations and Allied Documents: Travels and Explorations of the Jesuit Missionaries in New France, 1610–1791* (Cleveland: The Burrows Brothers Co. 1896–1901).

COMBING THE SNAKES FROM ATOTARHO'S HAIR

Native Stories of Natural Balance and Reconciliation

It has been the observation of many who have been intimately involved with the original Native cultures of North America that, although conflict and confusion are as much a part of the human experience among American Indians as among other peoples on this planet, such conditions are regarded by Native Americans as aberrations, as imbalances which should be righted. The right and "normal" state of affairs—in the traditional Native view—is balance and reconciliation, even after the most cataclysmic of imbalances.

The point might be made linguistically. The meanings of the words people use reveal something of their worldview. Among the Dineh, the nation popularly known as the Navajo, the word *hozho* appears again and again in their healing chants. It has frequently been translated to simply mean "beautiful," as in the often cited "Prayer of the Night Chant" (from which the phrase "House Made of Dawn" was taken to be the title of N. Scott Momaday's Pulitzer Prize–winning novel) rendered by the turn of the century anthropologist Washington Matthews to end:

> May it be beautiful before me
> May it be beautiful behind me.
> May it be beautiful below me.
> May it be beautiful above me.
> May it be beautiful all around me.
> In beauty it is finished.[1]

However, in Dineh, *hozho* does not mean just beauty. It also means "balance." Thus, this healing chant, which is only one component in a complex ritual of several days including group participation, singing, storytelling and the creation of a sandpainting which depicts one episode from the *Dine Bahane* (the epic creation story of the Navajo), indicates to us that balance is a beautiful and desirous condition, a state of health.

Similar ideas are found among the Haudenosaunee, those people commonly known as Iroquois, in the northeastern woodlands area of the continent. Among the Iroquois, the basic premise of medicine is that balance must be restored. As Daniel E. Moerman says in *Geraniums for the Iroquois: A Field Guide to American Indian Medicinal Plants:*

> The Iroquois, for example, have a highly complex theory of illness. For the Iroquois, illness was the tangible consequence of an imbalance of some sort in the patient's system.[2]

Such themes of balance relating to health are found not only in reference to human health and mental balance but to the health of the biosphere which surrounds us, to Earth itself. Further, political and social balance, relations between family members, between the people in a given nation and (in some cases) between nations of people are also regarded as the healthy and intended conditions of humanity. If balance and the restoration of balance are such central themes in North American Native life, where can we look to find the clearest expressions of such principles as well as, perhaps, ways in which the principles of reconciliation may be put into play in human life? We need look no further than Native oral traditions.

In his eloquent essay on the oral tradition entitled "The Man Made of Words," the Kiowa writer N. Scott Momaday comments on the "nature and possibilities" of storytelling. "Storytelling," he says, "is imaginative and creative in nature."[3] By telling stories, we are able to understand our experience. In fact, "the possibilities of storytelling are precisely those of understanding the human experience." (At a spring 1991 lecture at Skidmore College in Saratoga Springs, New York, the Nigerian novelist, Chinua Achebe, made a strikingly similar statement when he said, "We create stories and stories create us. It is a rondo.")

▲▼▲

Gluskabe is one of the central characters in the stories of the Penobscot nation. A trickster figure who is vastly powerful but often innocent of the results of his actions—he is a perfect metaphor for the power of the human beings affecting the balance of the natural world. His grandmother, Woodchuck, is wise with that knowledge of the earth needed to preserve things for "their children's children."

The anthropologist Frank G. Speck collected a number of such teaching tales from elderly Penobscot men and women, including Newell Lion, Hemlock Joe, Peter Nicolar, Newell Francis, Sarah Paul and Alice Swassion, people from the same community as Thoreau's guide, Joe Polis. In one of those stories, Gluskabe goes fishing and tricks all of the fish in the world into entering his fish trap by saying to them: "The ocean is going to run dry. The end of the world is coming and all of you will die. Enter in my river, and you shall live, because my river will always remain. Now, all who hear me, enter."

However, when Gluskabe shows his grandmother what he has done, her response is not praise—as one might expect from an elder in a culture which supposedly had no idea of the dangers of extermination or of the importance of natural balance. Instead, Grandmother Woodchuck says, "Grandson, you have not done well. All the fish will be annihilated. So what will our descendents in the future do to live?" As a result of her wise words, Gluskabe releases the fish from his trap.[4]

▲▼▲

A story told to George Bird Grinnell in the late 1800s by the old Pawnee warrior, Eagle Chief, the primary source for Grinnell's book *Pawnee Hero Stories and Folk Tales,* is an example of the awareness the Pawnee had that the seemingly endless buffalo herds which they relied upon for survival were to be hunted in a respectful and a measured fashion—not killed to the last animal as was done by European hunters. The tale is called "Ti-ke-wa-kush, The Man Who Called the Buffalo." In it, a man uses his own special power to help his starving people because when he "looked at the little children crying for something to eat … it touched his heart." He uses his power to call the buffalo, offering a sacrifice of "eagle feathers, and some blue beads, and some Indian tobacco." After four days, the people "saw a great buffalo bull come up over the hill to the place. He stood there for a short time and looked about, and then he walked on down the hill and went galloping off past the village. Then the man spoke to the people and said, 'There. That is what I meant. That is the leader of the buffalo; where he went the herd will follow.'"

Sure enough, just as Ti-ke-wa-kush promises, the buffalo come close to the village. The people surround them and kill many animals for food. However, the man tells them several things. For one, "In surrounding these buffalo you must see that all the meat is saved. *Ti-ra'-wa* (the "Creator") does not like the people to waste the buffalo." He also tells them, "Be careful not to kill a yellow calf—a little one—that you will see with the herd or its mother." Further, they are told that there must be an end to their killing, "You are to make one more surround and this will be the end."[5]

As with the Penobscot story, the good of the people is foremost, and wildlife is seen as the natural supplier of human food, but it is a supply which must be used wisely and never completely exhausted. Respect and balance are central principles for the health of the biosphere.

▲▼▲

Charles Alexander Eastman's Indian name was Ohiyesa, and he was born a Santee Sioux in Minnesota. After the so-called Sioux Uprising of 1862 separated him from his father, Eastman was raised in the forests in the traditional Sioux way. When he turned fifteen, two strangers reappeared in their camp—Indians in the clothing of the whites. One of them was Eastman's father, and he took his son with him back into the white man's world. There, Charles Eastman received a Western education which took him through Dartmouth University and medical school in Boston. His first job was as physician at the Pine Ridge Reservation, where he witnessed the events that led to the Wounded Knee Massacre and was the first doctor to go to the site of that mass killing of Sioux people to rescue the few survivors who remained. From that point on, Eastman spent the rest of his life trying to help his fellow Indians survive by learning the ways of the white world while holding on to the best of the Native cultures. In 1894 Eastman went to work for the YMCA and founded the YMCA camping experience, which introduced the American Indian land and conservation ethic into camping for the first time.

One of Eastman's best-known books is the 1902 recounting of his childhood in the woods, *Indian Boyhood*. In it, a number of traditional tales are told the young Ohiyesa by the elderly storyteller Smoky Day. What Ohiyesa receives is an education that Eastman saw in his later years to be even more relevant than his university degrees. Each story contains lessons, but none are more memorable or appropriate to teaching the central importance of the natural balance than the story of the Stone Boy. The Stone Boy is a powerful being who, at first, plays a hero's role. He valiantly rescues his lost uncles, doing great deeds for his people. However, halfway through the story something happens. The Stone Boy apparently becomes overwhelmed with his own power and falls into the trap of pride. He begins to kill animals wantonly:

> ... bringing home only the ears, teeth and claws as his spoil, and with these he played as he laughingly recounted his exploits. His uncles and his mother protested and begged him to at least spare the lives of those animals held sacred by the Dakotas, but Stone Boy relied on his supernatural powers to protect him from harm.

At last, the animal people gather together and decide they must join forces to destroy their enemy before he wipes them all out. Stone Boy uses his great powers, but the forces of nature are too great for him to overcome. The beavers dam the rivers, and the gophers and badgers dig under the great wall which Stone Boy has created to defend himself and his relatives. His misdeeds, by upsetting the natural balance, have doomed not only himself but his family as well. Finally:

> ... the water poured in through the burrows made by the gophers and the badgers and rose until Stone Boy's mother and ten uncles were all drowned. Stone Boy himself could not be entirely destroyed, but he was overcome by his enemies and left half-buried in the earth, condemned to never walk again, and there we find him to this day.
>
> That was because he abused his strength and destroyed for mere amusement the lives of the creatures given him for use only."[6]

Though it hardly needs restating, the theme of human beings destroying themselves and their kin by callous disrespect for nature is currently being acted out in the events in each day's newspaper—from a nuclear meltdown at Chernobyl to burning oil wells in the Persian Gulf.

▲▼▲

The themes of political and social balance can be seen with great clarity in certain of the most central oral traditions of the Iroquois, a League of Six Nations which banded together in response to the need for balance and reconciliation after a time of great strife. As Oren Lyons, one of the current chiefs of the Onondaga, the central "fire-keeping" nation of the Iroquois, explained to me many years ago (and attempted to explain to Bill Moyers in the television interview aired in July 1991), the Creator gave people certain original instructions. Central to those instructions was the admonition that they would live together in peace and mutual respect. However, as thousands of years passed, the people forgot those original instructions and began to war with each other. The blood feud, in which a death for a death was the order of the day, was common between the Mohawk, Onondaga, Cayuga, Seneca and Oneida.

It was then that the Creator renewed that original instruction by sending a messenger who became known as the Peacemaker. He traveled among the warring nations, bringing them peace. There were two people by his side. One was a great orator, a Mohawk chief known as Ayonwentha, whose name means "He Who Combs." (Longfellow misused his name, which can also be spelled Hiawatha, in his epic poem *Hiawatha,* which actually recounts the story of the Chippewa trickster hero, Manabozho. In Longfellow's defense, he took the word of the scholar Henry Rowe Schoolcraft who told him that Hiawatha and Manabozho were one and the same. But they are not. Confusing their names is a bit like mixing up Paul Bunyan with George Washington.) The other was a woman leader of the Neutral nation whose name was Jigonsaseh, the "Lynx." A central part of that story, which Oren Lyons related to Bill Moyers, is the episode concerning the restoration of balance to the chief of the Onondaga, a vastly powerful man known as Atotarho (also commonly spelled Tadodaho).

Atotarho's mind is so twisted, because of his love for power and his abuse of that strength, that snakes grow from his hair. His body has seven great crooks in it. At first he is so strong that the Peacemaker and Hiawatha and Jigonsaseh are unable to approach him. It is only when they create a song, based on the songs of the birds, that they are able to overcome Atotarho's magic. The song is so beautiful that it charms Atotarho, and he sits quietly, allowing them to come close. Then they straighten the crooks out of his body and Hiawatha combs the snakes from his hair. His mind has now been healed, and in recognition of the power which he now has which can be used for good, Atotarho is set up as one of the central leaders of the new League of the Iroquois, a League of Peace.

As Oren Lyons explained to me then, "We believe that the very worst of us can be made good." It is a philosophy of healing and reconciliation which is vastly different from the confrontational politics of the world stage or the endlessly repeated themes of revenge and killing your enemies which are the central stuff of much of our popular culture—books, movies and television.

Within these Native stories of balance and reconciliation we even find stories of how to survive the ultimate imbalance of all—the destruction of the earth. The present global ecological crisis is not at all unfamiliar or unexpected to many Native Americans whose prophecies and traditions tell of similar events in the far distant past and which speak of the coming of this present time of chaos which I have heard called the "Time of Purification" by some Native people. Within the oral traditions we find stories which give us a picture of a world thrown into chaos by wrong human actions, a world moving toward a holocaust. The traditions of the Pueblo, Hopi and Navajo peoples of the Southwest contain numerous examples of this. Those traditions say that our present world is either the Fourth World or the Fifth World. The previous worlds were wiped out by fire or by flood as a result of things done wrong by Coyote, the trickster figure who embodies (among other things) human appetites and human potential to make mistakes.

In Paul Zolbrod's 1984 rendering of the Navajo creation story, the *Dine Bahane,* we find the story of how the Fourth World is destroyed by flood after Coyote steals the two children of *Teehooltstodii,* the big Water Creature. The beings of the Fourth World escaped by planting a big reed which carried them up to the current world. However, when they looked back into the hole through which they came (that hole is found in every Pueblo *kiva* and is called the *sipapu*), they saw the water rising. It was then that they realized something was still wrong. They had to take action. When *Altse hastiin,* "First Man," looked at Coyote, Coyote looked down at his own feet:

"There," said he, "that's the rascal to blame. Something is wrong with the way he's been behaving. He never takes off his robe. Even when he lies down. I have been watching him ever since we arrived here. And now I am sure that he has something hidden under that cloak of his."

They searched Coyote and:

Sure enough, two strange looking creatures dropped to the ground. They looked something like tiny buffalo calves, except that they were covered with spots of different colors. They were the babies of *Teehooltstodii,* the big Water Creature: his very own children stolen by *Ma'ii,* the Coyote.

At once the people ran over to the island and threw the infants into the hole from which they had emerged. And in an instant the waters inside stopped welling and surging. With a deafening roar they were drawn back to the lower world.[7]

Although wrong actions resulted in the loss of the previous world, the new world turns out to be the most beautiful of all, as the people work together to make it so. It was in this last world that the light of the sun first shone and that the moon and the stars gave light to the darkness. As a parable for contemporary human beings, it is particularly telling. If this is a "Time of Purification," in which things look bleak because of the imbalance we have caused, then the possibilities of restoring that balance do indeed exist. By seeing things in that light, then we may work toward restoration, rather than retreat into despair or inaction because the task is too great. But, as the stories tell us, our first step is to recognize that which is out of balance—to cease being blind to the results of our deeds as Gluskabe was before Grandmother Woodchuck opened his eyes, to identify the cause of our troubles and then do what must be done—as did First Man when he returned the Water Babies. Only then, following the light of the stories, can we make this new world a balanced world, a brighter and a better one.

Notes

1. Washington Matthews, *Navajo Myths, Prayers and Songs* (Berkeley: University of California Publications in Archaeology and Ethnology, vol. 5, 1907).
2. Daniel E. Moerman, *Geraniums for the Iroquois: A Field Guide to American Indian Medicinal Plants* (Algonac, MI: Reference Publications, 1982).
3. N. Scott Momaday, "The Man Made of Words," in *The Remembered Earth,* Geary Hobson, ed. (Albuquerque: Red Earth Press, 1979).
4. Frank G. Speck, "Penobscot Tales and Religious Beliefs," *The Journal of American Folklore,* vol. 48, No. 187 (January–March 1935), 1–107.
5. George Bird Grinnell, *Pawnee Hero Stories and Folk Tales* (New York: Forest and Stream Publishing, 1889).
6. Charles A. Eastman, *Indian Boyhood* (New York: McClure, Phillips, 1902).
7. Paul G. Zolbrod, *Dine Bahane: The Navajo Creation Story* (Albuquerque: University of New Mexico Press, 1984).

SEEKING OUT THE REAL ROOTS

✪

Two Not-So-Simple Songs

I was asked, in 1992, when I was doing a program in an elementary school, to say something about the relationship between Native American music and European music. It was the year of the five hundredth anniversary of the arrival of Columbus in the Western Hemisphere, and people were asking all kinds of questions about the influence of European culture on the original peoples of the Americas. I answered that question with two songs.

The first one was this one. Just about everyone knows how it goes: "One little, two little, three little ..."

Then I paused. Of course, the people who were listening found it easy to fill in the missing word. "Indians," they sang.

But what did that children's song have to do with the question? Everything. It is a song which goes to the root of the misunderstandings brought to this "New World," which had ancient civilizations and sophisticated cultures for thousands of years before the first official arrival of Europeans in the Caribbean islands at the end of the fifteenth century. (Europeans, by the way, did not discover us. We weren't lost. Imagine someone from another country coming to your door and telling you, in a language you don't know, that they now own your house because they just found it!) Yet that song refers to the Native people of the Americas as "Indians," people whose continent is Asia. And it refers to them as "little Indians," a reference which may seem innocent, but is in fact demeaning and depersonalizing.

Even the beat of "One Little, Two Little, Three Little Indians" is a ridiculous parody of Native music, a music which has been so misunderstood that most people, when asked about "American Indian music," think of the stereotyped tom-tom drumbeat heard in an old Western movie whenever the danger of Indian attack is imminent, or the so-called "Indian chant" you could hear being sung, in 1995, on television as baseball fans cheered on the Atlanta Braves and the Cleveland Indians in their charge for the pennant. You know what I mean. You can hear it in your mind even as you read these words.

What is needed, I believe, is to start again, seek out the real roots. People need less to know about Columbus and his deeds than to know that before he and other Europeans came there were *people* here, people and cultures as deserving of respect as any in the world. Americans need to know that and also that, though centuries have passed, Native people and Native cultures *still* remain.

To understand something of what was here before Columbus, and is still here in the surviving Native peoples of the Americas and in their cultures, we must look to those real roots. And music is a good place to begin. We need to look at real Native American music or, I should say, musics. More than four hundred different languages were spoken in North America in 1492, and each language carried its own musical tradition, none of them at all like the boom boom boom boom, boom boom boom boom monotony of Indian music in those incredibly inaccurate Hollywood Westerns. (In one of the "classics," *She Wore a Yellow Ribbon*—which seems to be aired on TNT an average of once a week—we are treated to the sight of a line of female white actors depicting Indian woman playing that familiar one-two-three-four beat on what John Wayne calls a "medicine drum," banging sticks on a long wooden log rather like a New Guinea slit drum. This is far removed, indeed, from the truly sacred elk-skin drums actually played by the people of the plains. It is the equivalent of passing off as a Catholic mass a scene in which someone robed like a Buddhist monk—played, perhaps, by an Andaman Islander—bites off the head of a chicken.)

▲▼▲

Music is not separated from everyday life among Native peoples. It was said among many of the original Native nations that every person has a song, and songs were used not only for entertainment, but to preserve knowledge and help in daily tasks and in ceremonies. Though some songs were meant just to be sung, many others were always a part of a whole complex of dances and ritual activities. Beginning to understand Native music means beginning to understand the holistic nature of Native life. The world is regarded as powerful, and so songs were seen as instruments to make things happen. Sing a Lakota buffalo song, and buffalo will appear. However, responsibility goes with power. That song would only be sung under the right conditions and when there was a need for the buffalo. Similarly, the rain dances and accompanying songs of the Pueblo peoples would only be done in their own lands and at the time of year when rain was needed and conditions were right. And the dances would never be done for material gain, but for the good of the community. That is one reason why Pueblo people shake their heads when asked if they would come to some drought-stricken part of the country such as California, for money, to perform a rain dance. "They just don't get it," my old friend Swift Eagle once said.

▲▼▲

I recommend, as a good introduction to authentic traditional North American Native music, the four-cassette teaching package *American Indian Music for the Classroom* by the Creek composer, Dr. Louis Ballard. That set is available from Canyon Records, 4143 North 16th Street, Phoenix, AZ 85016 (602-266-4823), which also has a mail-order list of more than seven hundred different tapes of traditional and contemporary Native music from many different tribal nations. Some of the contemporary singers, such as Floyd Red Crow Westerman (Lakota), A. Paul Ortega (Apache) and Joanne Shenandoah (Seneca), have tapes of contemporary music which are good to use in classrooms. Also, David Campbell, an Arawak songwriter living in Canada, has done several wonderful albums for children. A few scholars have begun to write of the important, though generally unacknowledged, influence which Native music has had on jazz and on country and western music. That topic is too large and complex to do more than mention here.

But I need to get back to the second song which I offered that day in answer to the question about the relationship between Native American and European music. It is an example of the almost invisible but pervasive influence on this continent of Native culture and of how often we do not understand what that influence has been. It is a song which has been heard by almost every child, and I am sure that both the children and the adults who sang it to them were probably puzzled by the lyrics, not knowing the origin of the song was from the Wampanoag and Abenaki people of what is now called New England. In the seventeenth century, an Englishman heard a Native mother singing this lullaby to her child. He inquired about its meaning and then did a rough translation into English, keeping the same tune. Here is my own version of a part of that song as it might have been sung in the Abenaki language:

Gawi dzidzis, dzidzis gawi
Gawi dzidzis abazi
Gawi dzidzis oligawi
Gawi dzidzis olegwasi

The melody of that song was so familiar that everyone in the classroom nodded their heads.

"Do you recognize it?" I said.

"Yes, it's Rock-a-Bye Baby."

"Ever wonder what that baby was doing in a tree?" I said. "Does anyone understand why that baby was hung up in a tree?"

Everyone shook their heads, including the teachers. I could see in some of their faces that this was a question that had been bothering them for a long time.

"Here's the English translation," I said.

Sleep thou, baby, baby, sleep thou
Sleep thou baby, within the tree
Sleep thou baby, have a good sleep
Sleep thou baby, have a good dream

The baby in this song, I explained, is strapped inside its cradleboard and hung from the branch of a tree. As the wind blows, the cradleboard swings gently and the baby sleeps. That is why that baby was in a treetop! It was because it was a Native child in its cradleboard. It is a lullaby about being cared for and at one with nature (and in the original, the baby does *not* fall, that's a European addition). Not only do the wind and the tree combine to lull the child to sleep, but the cradleboard itself stands for the natural world. The board the child rests on is the earth, and the protective half-hoop of wood over the baby's face (so that if the cradleboard should fall, the baby would be protected from injury) stands for the rainbow or the arc of the sky. Every other part of the cradleboard has its own symbolic meaning—which may vary from one Native nation to another—while the cradleboard affords physical warmth, security and protection for the child.

▲▼▲

"Gawi Dzidzis," the original "Rock-a-Bye, Baby," is a song which offers us an image of Native people caring for their children within a secure environment and in balance with the natural world from the very start of their lives. It may be one way to begin to give children of today a picture of who the Native peoples of this continent were and still are.

Take Two Coyote Stories and Call Me in Your Next Lifetime: Some Final Thoughts on Storytelling, Healing and Appropriation

It was a beautiful day at the Bay Area Storytelling Festival in Tilden Regional Park just outside of San Francisco. There were birds singing and the wind carried both its own music and the scent of the tall eucalyptus trees that arched over the field where I had just finished telling the cradleboard story. But the young Anglo woman who was standing in front of me was not hearing the birds or feeling the cooling breath of the wind at that moment. She was too angry for that. Too angry and too busy accusing me of stealing the story I had just told (and the song which I sang as part of the story) from her.

"I wrote you a letter telling you about that song two years ago," she said. "You never answered my letter. Then a few months later I read an article you wrote, in which you talked about that song, and you never acknowledged me!"

I listened, waiting for a moment in which I could say a word. But such moments can be few and far between when you are being confronted by an angry property owner who thinks they have caught you crawling out their window with their best silver in your bag. So I waited longer. I looked over her shoulder at the tent where I was supposed to perform again in five minutes, and I waited a little longer. I waited while she told me how she had researched Indian cradleboards and even carried one around with her now when she told that story. Finally she paused.

"I never got that letter," I said. "Could I ask you to sing the song to me as you learned it?"

"Way-away, dzidzis," she sang.

"Ohnh-honh," I said, "those are the vocables that I used to use in the song before I started using the words *kaa-wi dzidzis,* meaning 'sleep thou, baby.' How did you happen to learn it that way?" I asked, seeing that the light was still not seeping in to clear away her anger.

"I sang it just as I learned it from the Native American storyteller who taught it to me four years ago," she said emphatically.

"Was her name Dovie Thomason?" I asked.

"Yes," she said, surprised for the first time, "how did you know?"

"Because I taught that story and that song to her eight years ago."

▲▼▲

Possession, it is said, is nine-tenths of the law. I wonder if the ones who first made up that maxim had any other sort of possession in mind as well, such as being so convinced that you know someone else's culture that you feel you possess it more than they do, or feel as if you have been (shades of the psychic-channel surfers) possessed by the spirit of Indians of the past who are more real than those of today. (Ever hear of a book called *Return of the Bird Tribes* in which an Anglo named Carey told the world that he was in direct contact with the spirits of such departed American Indians as the founders of the Iroquois League and, thus, he knew much more about Iroquois people than did contemporary Iroquois? My Tuscarora friend, Rick Hill, reviewed the book as "bird droppings.")

Ownership. Who owns a story after it has been told? I was taught that many of our stories are meant to entertain, to teach, even to heal. Because of that, they must be heard and shared. But, these days, at a risk. A risk of the stories being, shall we say, misappropriated—a risk that was as unlikely in the old days as it would be today for a modern M.D. to have a patient in for a diagnosis, prescribe the medicine to cure their illness or perform the necessary operation and then, a week later, discover that former patient out doing the same diagnosing, prescribing and operating. I think of another Native storyteller from the West who no longer performs at storytelling festivals because so many of the people who came to them were taping his stories as he told them, and then adding them to their own repertoires without his permission, without acknowledging where the stories came from, even changing and reshaping them. Possession. Possessiveness. Dispossession.

I find myself for a moment flashing back to an old episode of the British TV show *Monty Python* in which John Cleese, as the highwayman Davey Moore who "robs from the rich, gives to the poor," suddenly realizes that the rich, when robbed, become poor and, thus, he must give them back their belongings. "This redistribution of capital is trickier than I thought," he says.

▲▼▲

A few years ago I got a phone call from a professional storyteller—a non-Indian. This storyteller had heard a summary of another of the traditional Abenaki stories I tell from someone else who had heard me tell it. The message of this story was so wonderful this storyteller said—who had never met me before—that he had written a rhymed poem retelling the story. He read it to me over the phone. I listened until the poem was finished.

"That's nice," I said. I was being polite.

"Isn't that wonderful?" the other storyteller said. "And I already have a contract to have it published as a book by a major children's publisher."

That was when I stopped being polite.

I explained about the way stories reflect not just the material aspects of our cultures, but also something deeper, which can only be described as spiritual. I talked about the specific knowledge about specific tribal traditions that is needed to tell such stories as they should be told. I explained that I had spent seven years learning that story before I ever wrote it down or told it in public. And I also said that I would not give either my blessing or my permission for the story to be published in the version I had just heard over the phone, well-meaning though it had been. Some things I said more than once, more than twice. It was hard to explain, perhaps, because there is this long American tradition of taking things from Native people without even thinking about it. But the other person listened—just as that storyteller at the Bay Area Festival eventually listened. The rhymed version of the story was not published and that storyteller—whom I now consider a friend—has in recent years made some very sensitive public comments about not appropriating Native American stories.

There is a great hunger in American culture for meaningful stories. We need new stories. Many of the old ones which were imported from Europe (like influenza, measles and smallpox) have taught us all the wrong things. Defeat your enemies, defend your property, slay all the monsters, make lots of wealth, marry the princess or the prince (or both?) and live happily ever after. Those are very scary messages to me, especially when we realize just how few of us survive to live happily ever after when we are trapped at the edge of such tales.

Those of us who are Native American writers and storytellers will continue to find that the stories we tell touch the hearts and the spirits of the people who hear them. They do need to hear such stories, and we do need to tell them. A Navajo acquaintance of mine, who is a traditional healer, told me that once he realized he had that gift he knew that he had to become a healer or he would become sick himself. Still, he tried to fight it. He had a career already in law enforcement. But he ended up being a healer. It was what he had been given to give. So the option of just stopping or just not telling our stories to any except a few may not be the option that is best to choose.

Our problem, though, is when that hunger for the healing in stories becomes blind possessiveness, acquisitiveness. At that same festival in California, Oyate Books, the publishers of *Through Indian Eyes,* had a table. People would come up to it and say "Do you have any Coyote stories? I need some Coyote stories." And Beverly Slapin, the cocompiler of *Through Indian Eyes,* would answer, "We have this book of Okanagan Indian Coyote stories told by Mourning Dove. We have this book of Navajo Coyote stories." And people would say, "No, I just need general Coyote stories." And Beverly would say, "We have this book of Okanagan Coyote stories told by Mourning Dove. We have this book of Navajo Coyote stories."

So we need to tell our stories and make it very clear what stories we are telling and where they come from. We need to defend them in the way, perhaps, that the Iroquois defended the Great League of Peace. Instead of defeating our "enemies" we need to clear the cobwebs from

their eyes and comb the snakes from their hair. As Oren Lyons, a contemporary Onondaga Faithkeeper, explained it to me, the Peacemaker
and Hiawatha placed an eagle on top of the tall white pine tree which
they planted to symbolize the league. That eagle would always be watch-
ful for dangers approaching. But the tree had four white roots which
stretched to all the directions. Anyone who was willing and patient
enough to trace those roots, to follow to the letter all the rules of the
league, could stand beneath that great tree's peaceful shade. Cutting that
tree down or putting a fence around it would, I am sure, seem equally
wrong to the elders who understood the true meaning of the peaceful
sharing and deep respect which that tree continues to symbolize. Perhaps, if we can keep the image of the Great Tree in our minds, we can
begin to find the stories and the songs of peace we all need to survive.

PART III

THANKING THE BIRDS

Horned Owl Finds a Wife

(A Penobscot Story)

As birds of the night, owls have sometimes been associated with monsters, witchcraft and the coming of death in many of the Native cultures of North America. Because the owl can see in the night, when human vision is limited, there is often an air of mystery connected with the owls. In Navajo stories in the American Southwest, human sorcerers may take the shape of an owl when they go out at night to do evil deeds. In the legends of the Okanagan people of the Pacific Northwest, the Owl Sisters are cannibal monsters which hunt for children. Some feel that this role of the owl as monster or sorcerer may have been strengthened after the coming of western Europeans, especially the Spanish, in whose traditions the owl is represented as a dark creature of the night. Before the fifteenth century, the traditional Native American view of the owl may have been more balanced. The Hopi *kachinas,* figures representing ancestors and natural forces which bring the rain, include two owl *kachinas,* and there are lighthearted stories at Zuni about Burrowing Owl tricking Coyote. A Cheyenne friend told me that, although owls are often seen in their stories as creatures associated with witchcraft and bad medicine, "sometimes an owl is just an owl."

The role of the owl is a complex one among the Wabanaki, the "Dawn Land" peoples of the Northeast. Although, in certain circumstances, the call of an owl might be an omen of ill fortune, owls were not always seen as bearers of bad tidings. Because *titgeli,* the "screech owl," often chose to nest close to the edge of Wabanaki villages and would give a distinctive call when someone disturbed it late at night, it was known in traditional lore as the village guardian, one who would give warning against dangerous intruders. When hunting, men often wore a cape with two ears on it to mimic the appearance of *kokohas,* the "horned owl," and thus disguised would be able to creep close to the deer or the caribou. *Wabikokohas,* the "snowy owl," is a name given to one of the heroes of the old stories, who defeats such monsters as the Great Hare or huge stiff-legged bears as big as hills—a description which sounds much like a hairy mammoth. The following story of an owl who falls in love with a young woman comes from the traditions of the Penobscot, one of the Wabanaki Nations of Maine.

▲▼▲

Long ago, Horned Owl lived in a great pine tree with his old aunt. He was lonely and went looking for a wife. He flew from village to village, looking for just the right person to marry. At last he came to a Penobscot village by the side of a river. As he sat in a tree by the river, a young woman came down to get water. As soon as Horned Owl saw her, he knew that she was the one he wanted as his wife.

This young woman, though, was very proud of herself. Her name was Flowing Stream and she thought there was no man in the whole world good enough to marry her. Her parents reminded her that now that she was grown she might think of taking a husband, but none of the young men in the village pleased her.

"That one is too fat," she would say or "That one is too tall," or "I do not like the way he wears his leggings."

Finally her father could stand it no longer.

"Daughter," he said, "tell us what it is that you want."

The daughter thought for a bit and then decided to ask for something that no one could do. That way she would be left alone.

"I will marry the first man who can spit into the fire and make it burn hotter."

Horned Owl heard all that from his perch in a cedar tree. He flew home to his old aunt.

"My aunt," he said, "I have found the one I want to marry, but she says she will not marry anyone unless they can spit in the fire and make it hotter."

Horned Owl's aunt scraped some of the resin from the bark of the pine tree.

"Put this in your mouth," she said. "Spit this onto the fire, and it will burn hotter."

Horned Owl flew back to the edge of the village where he disguised himself as a handsome young man. His two large tufts of feathers, however, still stuck up on his head. To cover them, he put on a two-eared cap.

Many young men had now tried to make the fire burn brighter by spitting into it, but all had failed. Then Horned Owl strode into the village. Everyone was impressed by the tall young man.

"I have heard that your daughter will marry a man who can make the fire burn hotter by spitting into it," he said to Flowing Stream's parents.

"That is true," they said.

"Then I will marry her," Horned Owl said. He walked to the fire and spat out some of the pitch he held in his mouth. Immediately the flames flared up brightly.

Flowing Stream, though, was suspicious.

"Take off your cap," she said, "Let me see what you look like."

At first Horned Owl refused, but soon everyone in the village insisted. As soon as he took off his cap, his two feathered ears could be seen.

"I said I would marry the first man who could do what I asked," Flowing Stream said. "But this is not a man!"

Horned Owl was so embarrassed he turned back into his own shape and flew quickly into the woods.

Now Flowing Stream decided that she did finally have to marry someone. But she wanted that person to be one who could care for her and her parents. "I will marry the man who brings in the most game by tomorrow night," she said.

Horned Owl, who was sitting again in the tree at the edge of the village, heard what she said. He was a great hunter, and he hunted all that night and into the next day. Then he changed himself into the shape of a young man again, but one with very long, thick hair this time. He combed his long hair over his feathered ears and came into the village with all the game he had caught.

Everyone was impressed. This young man brought in twice as much as any of the others. Surely he should marry Flowing Stream.

Flowing Stream, though, was suspicious again.

"This young man looks familiar," she thought. Then she called him over to her. "Come and sit by the fire with me," she said.

Horned Owl sat down next to Flowing Stream. The fire was very hot and soon he began to sweat.

"Push back your hair from your face," Flowing Stream said. "Then you will feel cool."

As soon as Horned Owl pushed his hair back, his two feathered ears sprung up again.

"Look." Flowing Stream said, "This is not a man at all. It is the same one who tried to trick us before."

Once again, Horned Owl flew off disappointed.

Now Horned Owl was very sad. He sat in the tree near the edge of the village and began to sing a lonesome song. He sang about what a fine young woman Flowing Stream was and how much he wanted to be with her. He sang about how sad he was to always be alone.

In her wigwom, Flowing Stream heard Horned Owl's lonesome

song and it touched her heart. What did it matter that he was different? He truly cared for her. She walked out into the forest and called to him.

"Horned Owl," she said, "I will marry you."

Then Horned Owl flew down to her, and they were married. Horned Owl hunted for her and her parents and was a good husband. They were still living together happily when I left them.

Use Cedar to Greet the Dawn

I've spoken in an earlier essay of the June morning many years ago when I sat with my Cheyenne brother, Lance Henson, on a mountain in the Wichita range in Oklahoma. We watched the sun rise over the plains and placed a handful of dry needles of Western cedar on the glowing embers of the fire we had kindled before dawn.

"It is," Lance said, "one of the oldest of our ceremonies. One of the first that we teach children. Climb to a high place and make a fire before dawn. When the sun rises, place cedar on the embers and then wash your hands and face with the smoke. Pray for your health and for the health and well-being of others."

As the cedar smoke swirled about us, the first light of that rising sun edged the land with a nimbus of crimson. Then shadows broke free and came rushing toward us, spreading over the land as they grew longer and longer. Those long first shadows of the new day raced up the sides of the mountain and washed over us. For a moment I thought I heard the voices of spirit people singing an old song to greet the day. Then the sun rose higher and the running shadows were gone, replaced by the darker, shorter shadows of the morning. Hearing that old song, we prayed for the new day.

▲▼▲

A few years later, I sat with Louis Littlecoon Oliver, a Muskogee elder, on a bench in Tahlequah, Oklahoma, outside the tourist village of Tsa-la-gi, a reconstruction of an old Cherokee town in the time before the coming of Europeans. My walk through Tsa-la-gi had depressed me. The Cherokee people who worked there were instructed to stay in character, to pay no attention to the visitors and to speak only in Cherokee. Because some of the Cherokee people who worked there could not speak much of their own language, many of them went through the day, it appeared, saying nothing at all.

As I sat there, I, too, said nothing. I felt as if my own voice had been taken. But Louis understood. He placed a hand on my shoulder.

"My old people," he whispered, a gentle Okie drawl in his voice, "they said if you was feeling really depressed you should go up to a hilltop. Sit under a big tree right on one of its roots and then make a little fire. After that fire's burned down, you put some cedar on the coals. Just wash your face and your hands in that cedar. When you come down that hill you'll be a new man."

Those words he spoke must have lasted no more than a minute by clock time. But as he spoke them, it was as if we were walking up to that hilltop together. We sat under that old pine tree and we made the fire. I felt its warmth on my face as it burned, and that warmth loosened the pain which had tightened about my heart. I watched the cedar needles fall on the embers, saw them curl and darken and then lift up green and brown smoke which grew thicker and paler as it rose. I closed my eyes as I lifted that smoke with my cupped hands.

When I opened my eyes again, I was sitting with Louis on that bench once more. Louis looked into my eyes, which were moist with tears. The smell of cedar was all around us.

"Now you can go there any time you need to from now on," he said.

And so can you.

> The mountain seen
> and the mountain known
> are not the same.
>
> One is the image
> held in the eye.
> The other is the knowledge
> gained in the climb.
>
> The mountains we carry
> inside are the same—
> the images held,
> the wisdom gained.

THANKING THE BIRDS

Native American Upbringing and the Natural World

✦

Thirty years ago, Swift Eagle, an Apache man, was visiting some friends on the Onondaga Indian Reservation in central New York. One day, when he was out walking, he heard the sounds of boys playing in the bushes.

"There is another one," one of the boys said. "Shoot it!"

When he pushed through the brush to see what was happening, he found that they had been shooting small birds with a BB gun. They had already killed a chickadee, a robin and several blackbirds. The boys looked up at him, uncertain of what he was about to do or say.

At that point, I am sure, there are several things which a non-Indian bird lover might have done. A stern lecture on the evil of killing little birds, the threat of telling the boys' parents for doing something which they had been told not to do or even a spanking might have seemed in order. Swift Eagle, however, did something else.

"Ah," he said, "I see you have been hunting. You must have been very hungry. Pick up your game and come with me."

Then he led the boys to a place where they could make a fire and cook the birds. He made sure that they said a thank you to the spirits of the birds before they ate them, and as they ate, he told them stories about the birds. It was important, he said, to be thankful to the birds for the gifts of their songs, their feathers, even their bodies as food. The last thing he said to them, which they never forgot—for it was one of those boys who told me this story many years later—was this.

"You know," Swift Eagle said, "Our Creator gave the gift of life to everything that is alive. Life is a very sacred thing. But Our Creator knows that we have to eat to stay alive. That is why it is permitted for us to hunt to feed ourselves and our people. So I understand that you boys must have been very, very hungry to kill those little birds."

▲▼▲

I have always liked that story, for it illustrates several things. Although there were hundreds of different languages spoken on the North

American continent in pre-Columbian times, although there was an equally wide range of customs and lifeways, there were many deep similarities between virtually all of the Native American peoples. One of the deepest was the continent-wide tradition of depending on the natural world for their survival on the one hand but respecting it and attempting to remain in a right relationship with it on the other. A friend of mine of Cherokee Indian descent, Norman Russell, is a poet, botanist and author of a book entitled *Introduction to Plant Science: A Humanistic and Ecological Approach* (West Publishing, 1975). "Ecological balance," he said to me, "is nothing new for the Native American. It was their way of life."

As the story about Swift Eagle shows, the ideas held by an Apache from the Southwest fit into the lives and traditions of Onondagas from the Northeast. Moreover, his method of dealing with children who had done something incorrect or out of balance was particularly Indian. Handsome Lake was a Seneca Iroquois visionary of the early 1800s. His teachings, which are called in English the "Good Message," were the basis of a revival of the spirit and the strength of the Iroquois at a time when the theft of land and the inroads of alcohol seemed to be leading them toward destruction as a people. He is still regarded by the Iroquois as a prophet whose words were given him by the Creator. The "Good Message" is still memorized and spoken in the longhouses of the Iroquois in New York State and Canada. It covers many subjects and takes several days. One of its sections deals with children. "Talk slowly and kindly to children," Handsome Lake says. "Never punish them unjustly."

"Someone who strikes a child," a Kwakiutl wood-carver from the Pacific Northwest said, "has to be a great coward. Children are so much smaller than adults." "My father never struck me," my own Abenaki grandfather told me. "Instead he would just talk to me." In short, though it probably did happen from time to time, corporal punishment of children was the exception rather than the rule among American Indian people of the past, and that approach of "sparing the rod" largely remains true today.

How, then, were Native American children taught the values of their culture, especially the value of living in balance with nature? Again, that story about Swift Eagle provides an example. Children were taught through example and through stories. Instead of scolding or lecturing them, he showed them how to build a fire and cook the game they had shot. Even though the game was little songbirds, he gave the same respect he would have given to a rabbit or a deer. He told them stories which pointed out the value of those birds as living beings. He had them give thanks to the spirits of the birds for allowing themselves to be killed. And he emphasized, gently but clearly, the importance of only taking the life of another living thing out of need.

In large part, Western education today tends to be didactic. From books, lectures, film strips and movies, we learn *about* things but rarely actually do them. We then test the knowledge which has been gained by having our students answer questions *about* the things they have "learned." There are, of course, good reasons for this. The world which our children must learn about is too broad for them to have a hands-on approach to everything. However, as many educators have observed, too often the result of such education is rote learning which is more of a conditioned reflex than a true understanding. Further, the artificial divisions between fields of knowledge—with natural science, alone, divided into botany, zoology, geology, astronomy and literally hundreds of other subdivisions and areas of study—can produce a situation in which your result is the kind of knowledge one gains in dissecting a frog. You know its parts, but you cannot put them together. And, in cutting it apart, you have killed that frog.

Native American education, on the other hand, has always tended to be experiential and holistic. People learn by doing things. If one wishes to learn how to make baskets, one goes to a person making baskets and watches them as they work. If you are patient and watch long enough, eventually that basket maker may ask you to do something, to hold onto this coil of sweetgrass here, to help shave down this strip of ash. Eventually, over a period of time, you discover that you, too, know how to make a basket. But making a basket is not all that you have learned. A basket maker has to know which trees and other plants can be used and at which times of year they can be prepared. Thus, a knowledge of botany and of the rhythms of the seasons is required. When cutting a tree or uprooting a clump of sweetgrass, a basket maker must give thanks to that plant for sacrificing its life to help human beings survive. Tobacco is left in exchange for that sacrifice. Thus, there is a religious component to basket making. There are stories, also, to be learned about the baskets, about the items used in their crafting, about the significance of patterns and designs that are a part of the basket. Among the Pima people, the figures of the whirlwind or the man in the maze appear on baskets and have stories connected to them which must be learned. There may even be songs. A Pomo woman basket maker once sang her basket song for me as she worked, explaining that it must be done a certain number of times in just such a way when making a basket. When the song ended, the basket was done. Thus, making a basket is not something to be easily learned out of a book. For American Indian basket makers (and, I am sure, basket makers in other traditional cultures), it involves much more than just simple handcraft.

Children, as any sensible teacher knows, respond to doing things. Activities are almost always the favorite part of a day for a child in school. Imagine, then, a school made up of nothing but activities, and you may be able to better understand why this method of teaching was so widely practiced among Native American people. Children also respond to stories. A good story, in fact, is very much like doing something, for it takes the listener along and involves that listener in such a way that the events of the story come alive and the trials and accomplishments of the central character become those of the listener, who is more of a participant than a passive observer (as is the case with television). Going back to that story of Swift Eagle and the Onondaga boys, the ritual activity of making the fire, thanking the spirits of the birds, hearing those stories and then eating the game they had killed taught them more than a hundred stern lectures could have taught and has stayed with them all of their lives.

Ray Fadden, an elder whose Mohawk name is Tehanetorens, is the founder of the Six Nations Indian Museum in Onchiota, New York, at the northern edge of the Adirondack Park. He began using traditional Iroquois stories as a means of transmitting his beliefs about the natural world more than four decades ago and continued to use those stories during thirty-five years of teaching Indian and non-Indian students in public schools in New York State. When he began teaching, many Native American people were turning away from their heritage. The old stories which taught people respect for nature and also showed them how to enjoy it more deeply seemed to be disappearing. Ray Fadden began to learn and make use of those stories. The more he used the old tales, the more his students responded. He became known as one of the foremost experts on the history of his Iroquois people and began recording legends and traditions in beaded belts which he made himself, drawing on the forms of the wampum record belts of past centuries. Eventually he built the Six Nations Museum, without the help of any governmental or foundation funding. To this day, though he has retired from the public schools, with the help of his son, Kahionhes, he keeps the museum open to the public through the warm months of the year. On any given day during what he calls "the tourist season," he may be found reading one of those belts which tell such old stories as that of the brave hunters who followed the Great Bear up into the Sky Land, or the more recent tale of the damaging of the chain of life which began with the destruction of natural habitat and the extermination of natural species as he explains conservation as the Indian saw it, an ecologically sophisticated view of the interrelatedness of all beings which his old stories indicate were a part of the Iroquois way for countless generations. As was the case when he was a teacher, his stories are first and foremost for the children. "You youngsters get in here and sit right down. I have a story that you need to hear." But anyone who sits and listens quickly realizes that such stories are for young and old alike.

"Stories," Tehanetorens explains, "were the first thing used to correct a child when they did something wrong. If the lesson story didn't work, then water might be thrown into that child's face or they might be dunked. If that didn't work, then the last thing, which always worked, was to pretend that child just didn't exist. They learned pretty quickly then that they had to mend their ways.

These stories are so strong that they were only to be told in the wintertime when Mother Earth is asleep. If the stories are told during the summer then the other creatures might hear you and neglect their work. That's how strong these stories are."

▲▼▲

When Tehanetorens first taught in Indian schools in New York State, the idea of imbuing children with traditional Iroquois values or even using Indian storytelling as a part of a school curriculum was unthought of or forbidden. Western concepts of education have been so foreign to American Indian students—with the emphasis placed on didacticism and the Western tendency to depersonalize the universe—

that it is no surprise that schools have been a hostile environment for all too many American Indians. Today, thanks to work such as his, something closer to the old patterns of Indian teaching may be found within the walls of such institutions as the Onondaga Nation School in Nedrow, New York, in the heart of the Onondaga Reservation. A school run by the Onondaga community with the approval of the state education department, ONS makes use of old patterns in very special ways. Their Indian heritage is even honored by the school calendar, which provides a vacation for students and staff during the time of the Midwinter Ceremonials that come each year when the Dancing Stars—which Europeans call the "Pleiades"—are at the very height of the winter sky. During the time of the traditional Thanksgiving to the Maple Trees, when the sap is gathered in March, there is a maple festival at the school, and a sugarhouse is kept running out back, close to the school kitchen, cooking down the sap from trees tapped by the students. When it is the time to dig wild onions, a group of students and teachers gather during the day to go out into the fields around the school and harvest. In the bilingual classroom, supervised by Audrey Shenandoah, storytelling is one of the favorite activities in the room, and students from the preschoolers to those in the upper grades take part. The Onondaga students introduce themselves to a visitor by speaking their clan names and their Indian names in Onondaga. The walls and pillars of the basement room are decorated with paintings of animals and figures from Iroquois mythology. Looking at those pictures, of Wolf and Eel, Snipe and Bear and Deer, one sees that such Native American traditions as that of the "clan animals" create a sense of closeness to nature from birth, which most young people of European ancestry have never experienced. Among the Iroquois (and most other Native American peoples throughout the continent), you are born into a clan. In the case of the Iroquois, you inherit your clan from your mother. Each clan is represented by an animal (among some other native peoples, such natural forces as Sky or Wind may take the place of a clan animal), and you feel a particular closeness to it. Just as the majority culture's ideas of astrology (enormously popular ideas, as often as they are debunked or scoffed at) indicate that you are affected by your star sign, so too, one's clan seems to have some effect on one's personality. I have often heard it said that members of the Bear Clan tend to be big, strong people, that those who are "Wolves" are quick moving and volatile, that "Turtles" are slow moving and careful. Certain traditional stories are associated with different clans. There is a Mohawk story, for example, of how the Bear Clan was given the secrets of medicine plants by the Creator. Throughout the continent there are "bear doctors," and it is said that bears suffer from many of the same sicknesses people do and that by watching what herbs a bear eats when it is sick, one may learn to cure certain human illnesses.

Having a clan animal with which one is intimately connected is only one way in which American Indian culture and stories create a sense of closeness to nature for Native children. The forces of nature are personified in ways which I feel to be essentially nonromantic and usefully realistic. The four winds, for example, are associated with certain animals. The north wind is called the "White Bear" by certain American Indian nations. It is strong and cold and brings the snow. The east wind is called the "Moose" by the people of the northern maritimes. They see it walking out of the water with its great strength and shaking the moisture from its wide antlers. The south wind is the gentle "Fawn." When it arrives it comes with the warmth, the new flowers, the green grass. The west wind is the "Panther," striking with sudden force. Such names accurately describe the characteristics of these winds, are easy to remember and also make the forces of nature—because they are better understood in the shapes of animals—less threatening.

Even the calendar is seen differently through the eyes of American Indian culture and stories. Instead of learning the names of the months of the year through the old rhyme "thirty days has September, ..." American Indian children are still, through their elders and in schools such as ONS, taught the thirteen moons. Each moon is named according to some event taking place in nature at that time of year. The time around November is, for the Abenaki, *Mzatonos,* the "Moon of Freezing," the time around October is *Pebonkas,* the "Moon of Leaves Falling," and around May is *Kikas,* "Planting Moon." Each Native people has its own names for the moon cycles, names which reflect the condition of the natural world and also remind the human beings of the activities they should be undertaking.

I can never think of the cycles of the year without seeing the Turtle's back in my mind. In the stories of a good many Native American people—from California to Maine—the earth was built on the back of the Great Turtle who agreed to support the world. A St. Francis Abenaki elder and teacher of mine, Mdawelasis, once told me the stories connected with the Turtle's back.

"Count the number of squares on the Turtle's back," he said. "You'll see there are always thirteen. That is how many nations there were of our Abenaki people. Turtle remembers when others forget."

Then he went on to show me how the Turtle's back is also a calendar. There are thirteen squares, and there are thirteen moons. Around those large plates on the back of the Turtle there are always twenty-eight smaller plates. That is how many days there are in every moon. "There are stories in everything around us," he said. "You just have to know how to look in order to see them."

One of my favorite Abenaki stories is that of Gluskabe's Game Bag. It is a tale I have frequently told to students and used in workshops on storytelling and the Indian view of ecology. Gluskabe is the transformer hero of tales told by the different Abenaki Nations, from the Passamaquoddy of Maine to the St. Francis Abenaki of Vermont. In the story, Gluskabe goes hunting but is not successful. Angered, he goes to his grandmother and convinces her to make him a magical game bag, which will stretch to fit anything placed within it. He then goes into the woods and places the bag in the middle of a clearing. Then he begins to weep and moan. The animals come out and ask him what is wrong. "It is too awful," he says. "I cannot tell you." Finally, though, he does. "The world is going to be destroyed," he says. Now the animals become afraid. "What can we do?" they say. "Ah," says Gluskabe, "you can hide in my game bag." Then all of the animals in the world, even the great bears and the moose, climb into the game bag and Gluskabe ties it shut. He has caught all the animals now. Then he takes them home. But his grandmother sees the game bag is very full and says, "What do you have there, Gluskabe?" "Nothing," he says. But she persists, and he opens the game bag so she can look in. There are all the animals in the world looking up at her. "Now," Gluskabe says, "we no longer have to work to hunt. We can just reach into the game bag for food." But his grandmother shakes her head. "This is wrong," she says. "Animals cannot live in a game bag. And what about our children and our children's children? If we have all the animals now, what will they have to eat?" Then Gluskabe sees he is wrong. He goes back into the forest, opens the game bag and says, "All you animals, come out. The world was destroyed, but I put it back together again." Then the animals come out and go back into the forest.

Today, when the secrets of Gluskabe's magical bag, which can catch and destroy all of the animals of the world, are known all too well, it is important for such stories to be told. The teachings which have been given to generations of Native American children by such stories are ones which need to be understood not just by Indian people but by all of us. For ourselves and for our children's children.

STEALING HORSES

❉

Those non-Natives who have lived closest to the Indian have often been amazed at the absence of theft in Native American communities. A contemporary observer of Native ways, Richard Erdoes, wrote in his book *The Sun Dance People,* which deals with the Plains Indians and especially the Sioux:

> Among a people without locks, keys, or money, there were no thieves. ... Without lawyers, contracts, or anything in print, men found it impossible to cheat. Without jails there could be no criminals.[1]

Yet if those observations are true, what about stealing horses? The picture of the nineteenth-century Plains Indian as a "horse thief" is one of the few images of American Indians firmly fixed in popular culture which is basically correct. The Native people of the Plains prided themselves on being great horse thieves and honored those who stole many horses. Further, if there were no thieves, why does theft occupy such a central place in so many Native American folk stories? There are at least as many instances of American Indian culture heroes engaging in acts of theft as there are in the classical myths of the Western world.

Part of the answer to those questions may be found in that quote from Erdoes. Ideas of acquiring more wealth and personal property than ones needs—becoming a Donald Trump—so common in America, so connected with image and status, were foreign to the Native American. Do not think, by any means, that this was because Indians were saintly and unconcerned with how others saw them. Quite the contrary was true, for it is hard to imagine people more aware of their image in the eyes of their people, their honor and their status than Native Americans—past and present. But the orientation of accomplishment was toward the group rather than the individual, benefiting the people rather than one person. A man of great wealth who did not share freely was not respected. A reporter from the East once asked Sitting Bull why his people looked up to him.

"Is it not true," Sitting Bull said, "that in your country people look up to a man because he has much land, owns many horses and is very rich?"

"Yes," the reporter answered.

"Well," Sitting Bull said, "my people look up to me because I am so poor."

The person who did something so purely for one's self that it became antisocial—such as stealing personal property from a member of one's own tribal nation—was committing a double transgression. Not only was he stealing, he was placing his own personal interests above those of the people. The punishment for such an offense was often the most devastating sort of punishment imaginable to the group-oriented Indian—to be sent into exile.

On the other hand, taking things from one's enemies was not an antisocial act. Quite the contrary, when one considers that in many cases the first thing a successful horse thief would do would be to give away many of his newly acquired horses to others. As Erdoes puts it: "Warriors stole horses from their enemies, but of these deeds of war a man could be proud."

Warfare, before the whites came and changed all the rules, was in many ways a sacred game between many Native American nations. Its objective was not so much the destruction of an enemy people or the obtaining of their land (though hunting territories were often fiercely contested and the smaller nations such as the Cheyenne had to be great warriors to survive with enemies on all sides of them) as it was to protect one's people and win individual honor. Connected to the practice of counting coup (touching an enemy in battle or doing something similarly brave), stealing horses was a praiseworthy exploit. Two Leggings, a Crow warrior, in telling the story of his life (as related in Peter Nabokov's *Two Leggings: The Making of a Crow Warrior*) listed the four most important coups. Cutting an enemy's horse from the door of his tipi was second only to striking an enemy in battle. A horse was one of the few things which the people of the plains saw as "private property," and a man's favorite horse, tethered at night by a rope which led through the tipi door to the wrist of its owner, was not an easy thing to take. In fact, spiritual help was quite often sought by those who attempted such daring exploits. (In the case of Two Leggings, a famous medicine man named

See the Living Bull gave the young warrior-to-be special dreams to guide him on his raids for horses.)

The preparations for such horse-stealing raids were accompanied by ceremonial practices and even taboos among many Native peoples. According to LaVerne Herrall Clark's book, *They Sang for Horses,* this was especially true among the Athapascan people of the Southwest. Apache and Navajo raiders purified themselves for four days in the ceremonial sweat lodge before going on a raid. Sexual restrictions were placed upon them when they went through their preparations. Sacred songs, such as those taught to the Wind and Sun People by Monster Slayer, were sung.

This special care for their state of spiritual preparedness did not end when the raid began. Powerful amulets and talismans were carried with them. An altered language was used by both Apache and Navajo when on a raid. For example, the horses they intended to capture would not be referred to by their ordinary name but called "a live one's plume." (In *Navaho Religion,* Reichard says that this is "a circumlocution flattering to the horse and signifying its identification with supernatural speed and lightness."[2]) This special language was never spoken in their own country, because it was believed using it would bring an attack from their enemies. While on the trail, they had to control their thoughts, as thinking of unpleasant things might make them happen. The Jicarilla Apache even placed a taboo on scratching one's self with one's fingernails while on a horse raid, and so they carried special scratch sticks of pine or cedar carved into the shape of a horse's hoof. Among the Apache, the wives of the men of the raid also had to observe such restrictions as not bathing or eating salt while their husbands were gone. They ate and drank as sparingly as their husbands were then eating and drinking. All of their actions had to be as cautious and circumspect as those of a man in enemy territory.

While the ceremonies connected with horse stealing may not have been as elaborate among the peoples of the plains, they made a ritual of horse stealing, too. John Stands-in-Timbers writes about it in his autobiography, *Cheyenne Memories,* when he speaks of how Little Old Man, a Northern Cheyenne, prepared in 1855 for a raid on the Shoshones by the Cheyenne Fox Society. The society members were told by a crier to gather at a certain tipi wearing their finest clothing and ornaments, as if there was to be a dance. When they gathered, the man who invited them made a short speech about his desire to go on foot (as did most horse-stealing expeditions) to make a war trip against the Shoshones. That evening, those who wished to go on the war party gathered again, this time at the right end of the village, where they began singing the song of the Fox Society war chiefs. They walked through the village, singing, until they came to the tipi of the man who had proposed the war party. There, another kind of singing began:

> They called it singing wolf songs or love songs because they let their sweethearts know they were going out to do some brave things. After they reached the teepee they sang for a long time like that. The young men made beds around the outside and lay on their backs. Then the first one began singing a song about a girl, perhaps mentioning her name. The people all gathered to listen, and when the girl heard this she was glad and proud. After that he did not dare to change his mind or back out of what he had decided to do.[3]

Though it was a "sacred game," stealing horses was not for a man who was a coward or unskilled. Though people might celebrate those of their own people who stole from the enemy, if they caught an enemy stealing their horses, that thief was never treated lightly. Just how grim that risk was can be measured by a story I was told a number of years ago. Standing in the shadow of Taos Mountain, Joseph Concha nodded his head down across the fields.

"Down there in the cottonwoods," he said, referring to an incident more than a century ago, "is where they caught that Comanche horse thief. He came many times and took our horses. We knew it was the same man because he had a scar shaped like a half moon on the bottom of his left foot. You could see it in his prints. Finally, one night when he was trying to steal horses, someone saw him and he was wounded. The women followed his tracks and found him down there in those trees. They grabbed him by the arms and legs and pulled him apart."

A similar story of the dire fate of horse thieves who were caught is to be found in *Cheyenne Memories*. Not far from the present-day town of Busby, Montana, a party of Cheyenne buffalo hunters heard someone singing in the hills above them. It was a member of a Crow raiding party driving a large herd of captured Cheyenne horses. The buffalo hunters cut across and waited for the Crow raiders on the other side of the hill. Charging them at daybreak, they recaptured the herd and killed one of the Crows, a man whose hair was short. That place is still called by the Cheyenne the "Place Where the Short-Haired Crow Was Killed." Wolk Tooth, the grandfather of John Stands-in-Timbers, was in on that raid and used to sing the song which they heard that Crow raider singing.

So, though horse stealing was a game, it was played for the highest stakes. The Cheyenne raid against the Shoshone, which began with the young warriors singing their love songs, ended in death for six of the nine men who went, when they found themselves surrounded by the enemy. Only three escaped when the Shoshone, after losing three of their own men, pulled back from the fight because they did not know how many Cheyennes remained.

Such risks, of course, made horse stealing all the more honorable. Since the captured horses would be given to friends, relatives and those in need, the deed itself was at least as important as the horses taken. Success in a raid was not only proof of a man's courage and ability, it also indicated that he was blessed by spiritual guidance and good medicine, a person willing to risk his life for his honor and the good of the people. The old saying that someone is "a good man to steal horses with" had special meaning among Native Americans.

In a seeming contradiction to the unspoken understanding that one did not steal from one's own people, village boys would form raiding parties to purloin dried meat from the racks near the lodges in their own village. This, however, was neither an unorganized or an antisocial act, but an approved means of training young men in the stealth and nerve which would eventually be of benefit to their people.

In his autobiography, Black Elk, the famed Lakota medicine man, spoke fondly of doing this when he was a child and there is a wonderful description of such a meat-stealing raid in Frank Linderman's *Plenty-Coups: Chief of the Crows*. In it, several young boys are told by an old warrior to "steal" a wolf robe from their own lodges and meet him that night at the appointed place where there would be plenty of mud to darken their faces:

When we were all met we seated ourselves to listen to what he had to tell us. He did not mention meat. He called it horses and spoke in this fashion: "Young men, there is an enemy village near us. Our Wolves (scouts) have seen it and counted many fine horses tied near the lodges. To enter this village and cut a fine horse is to count coup. See! I have here some nice coupsticks." He held up several peeled sticks to which were tied breath feathers of a war eagle.[4]

Plenty-Coups is only partially successful in his attempt to steal "horses." He is caught by a strong old woman, who washes his face—both to show his friends that he has been caught and to see who the disguised marauder is. She then gives the boy the best piece of meat on the rack, but "I could not say I stole it, because my face was clean."

Something of the importance of being a good horse thief can be understood by realizing the importance the horse came to hold in the Plains Indian cultures. LaVerne Herrall Clark describes it well in *They Sang for Horses* when she talks of the impact these new animals had on the Apache and Navajo:

> The acquiring of the horse by the Southern Athapascans was of major importance to their lifeways. It brought mobility and freedom of movement to those semi-nomadic people who had previously known only the tedious foot journeys of a few miles a day with all their possessions loaded on their backs or loaded on slow packs of dogs. ... In Navajo and Apache societies, continual movements within defined territories were essential for their mode of subsistence. With horses, they could make their seasonal rounds carrying all their goods on pack horses while the entire family rode to the new camp in previously unknown comfort.[5]

In addition, the horse made contact possible with other peoples for wider, faster trade. The hunting of the buffalo was suddenly made much easier, and following the herds as they now could had been made possible by horses. As the buffalo became scarcer and scarcer when white incursions increased, it became impossible to hunt this animal, which was their mainstay, without their horses. Quite literally, the cultures of the Plains were reshaped around the horse. Even the tall tipis, now synonymous with the Plains Indians, were a recent innovation made possible by these strong new four-footed helpers who were able to drag the long tipi poles from place to place. Before the horse, Lakota tipis were much smaller, and many other nations which had stayed in one place and lived mostly as farmers now became seminomadic hunters with the coming of the horse. Soon it became clear that a nation with many horses was a strong nation. Those who stole horses for the people held their heads high.

Horse stealing, of course, is no longer practiced this way today, but some contemporary practices keep a kind of good-natured rivalry alive between Native American tribal nations. For example, there is "stealing the drum." Each summer, all across the continent, wherever there are Native people, an annual round of powwows begins. People gather to display and sell their crafts to the public, to sing and dance (often for big prizes) and get together for a good time. Drumming groups, which play social dance songs, may also compete with each other. Stealing the drum from another group is a way to both play a joke and "count coup" in a modern context. The "stolen" drum is eventually given back. The closest thing to this in Anglo culture is the custom, among college students, of trying to kidnap another school's mascot before a big football game.

I still can hear Barney Bush, the well-known Shawnee writer, laughing about the time he and a group of other students at the Institute of American Indian Arts in Santa Fe were able one year to "steal" the school drum which they then took up onto a hill above the town (in earshot of the school) for a loud impromptu powwow. On another occasion, he and a friend accompanied Harold Littlebird, the Pueblo poet and singer, to the airport after Harold had given a performance. Said Barney:

"He was carrying that drum he uses to accompany himself when he sings and we kept saying 'You go ahead and check on your flight. We'll just stay here and watch your baggage.' But he just held onto that drum of his and said 'That's all right.' He knew that if he took his eyes off that drum, it would have been gone."

If one of the motives in raiding horses was to provide for the people, then it is not a big jump from horse stealing to certain types of theft common in Native American traditional stories. In those stories, which speak of the great deeds of culture heroes, there can be found the purest examples of what the Western world might call "Promethean theft"— stealing for the good of the people.

The Southern Paiute people say that there was no fire in the world, and things were very hard for the human beings as a result. They were naked and shivered in the cold. The animals took pity on them, and Coyote went to steal fire from those who owned it but refused to share it. With the help of Crested Jay and various other birds and animals, he was able to bring the warmth and blessing of fire to the human beings. In a similar fashion, the Tahtlan and other people of the Northwest tell how Raven stole fire's light from the house of Daylight Man, who was keeping it all for himself while the rest of the world was in darkness. After he is successful, Raven says, "These things will never again belong to just one person or be locked up. They'll be for all the People." In the Northeast, the Abenaki people tell how Tobacco, which was intended to be a sacred plant (when used in the right way) for all of the people, was being kept by the magician Grasshopper. Gluskabe goes to steal Tobacco from Grasshopper. (In another story, Gluskabe also steals summer from the people who are keeping the rest of the world locked in the grip of winter by not sharing what they have.)

One of my favorite Iroquois stories tells of a group of hunters who encounter two Stone Giants, monsters who eat human beings. One of the Stone Giants has a magic pointing finger which shows the direction of whatever it is they are after when he places it on his palm and asks a question. One of the hunters climbs a tree and when the finger keeps pointing straight up after the Stone Giant asks, "Where is the one I am chasing?" the Stone Giant stands there in thick-witted confusion. (Stone Giants, though powerful, are notoriously dense—rather like the Bureau of Indian Affairs.) The hunter slips down the tree, steals the magic finger and flees. He then uses the finger to outwit the Stone Giants and, later, to find game animals for his people.

If there is one evil which is greater than others to Native people, it is selfishness. When someone owns something which could benefit others and does not share it, that is a great wrong—especially when that something is one of the great gifts, a gift like Fire or Light or Tobacco ... or Horses. When Native people first saw horses in the possession of the

Spanish, they thought they were as powerful and beautiful as something from the spirit world. To this day, the name for horse in some Indian languages is "Spirit Dog." (Before the horse, dogs were the primary pack animal, carrying things in bags or dragging them on travois poles.) Soon, the horse worked its way into the Creation myths. Among the Navajo and Apache, there were soon stories of how the horse was created for human beings by a culture hero or given to them by their deities, who had their own horses from the beginning of time, even before the coming of the Europeans. Horses, clearly, were meant for all the people.

Though the days of stealing horses may be gone forever and the once scarce blessings of Fire and Tobacco are all too easy for most of us to come by now, these stories of stealing horses and stealing for the people remain. The lessons they taught are as alive, today, as they were when the horse first stepped onto the Western plains several hundred years ago or when the world was in cold and darkness and only the fires of sharing made it possible for the people to survive.

Notes

1. Richard Erdoes, *The Sun Dance People: The Plains Indians, Their Past and Present* (New York: Alfred A. Knopf, 1972).
2. Gladys A. Reichard, *Navaho Religion: A Study of Symbolism* (n.p.: Books Demand UMI, repr. of 1963 ed.).
3. John Stands-in-Timbers and Margot Liberty, *Cheyenne Memories* (Lincoln: University of Nebraska Press, 1972).
4. Frank Linderman, *Plenty-Coups: Chief of the Crows* (Lincoln: University of Nebraska Press, 1962).
5. LaVerne Herrall Clark, *They Sang for Horses: The Impact of the Horse on Navajo and Apache Folklore* (Tucson: University of Arizona Press, 1966).

STRIKING THE POLE

Observations about Indian Humor

One of the most common European images of the Native American is that of the mirthless Red Man. As Arthur Parker, a Seneca writer, put it in *The Indian How Book* in 1927, "That the Indian was solemn in mien and never saw the humorous side of life has almost become a tradition." The truth, of course, was and is far different. To quote Parker again:

> Did the Indian ever joke, tell funny stories, play tricks, engage in humorous pranks, or roar himself sick over a funny situation? The only writers who ever said such things are those who never knew the joy-loving red man. Indeed, the Indians did joke, and the forest more often rang with their laughter than it did with their war whoops.[1]

Why, then, has the picture of the humorless Indian been so common in so much of the literature, in so many of the film and television depictions of Native Americans? Part of the reason may be that many of those people who wrote about Indians either knew them not at all (like the early twentieth-century German writer, Karl May, whose novels about American Indians remain favorites of German readers, even though May never visited America and drew his noble savages more from Fenimore Cooper than from real life) or were so without humor themselves that they failed to see its vital place in Native American life.

Not all of those who wrote about Indians were totally blind to the place of laughter in Native American lives. In 1882 Richard Irving Dodge published *Our Wild Indians—Thirty-three Years' Personal Experience among the Red Men of the Great West*. In it, he observed that the Indian is sometimes reserved and silent in the presence of strangers, but:

> In his own camp, away from strangers, the Indian is a noisy, jolly, rollicking, mischief-loving braggadocio brimful of practical jokes

and rough fun of any kind making the welkin ring with his
laughter.[2]

Although Dodge still appears to miss some of the point by ascribing
only a sort of crude humor to his "Wild Indians," he does at least understand that they are capable of laughing. I suspect, too, that Dodge may
not have recognized certain other kinds of humor which are common
among the Plains Indians and other Native Americans, humor which is
either so subtle or so keyed to an understanding from within of what is
funny to a people that an outsider would fail to recognize it. Anyone
who has made an ironic remark and had it taken completely seriously is
in the same situation that many American Indians have found themselves in when they've cracked a joke to a non-Indian and failed to get a
laugh.

▲▼▲

Robert Conley, a Cherokee friend of mine, and I once planned to
put together an anthology of Native American humor. I mentioned our
idea to N. Scott Momaday, the Kiowa writer whose first novel, *House
Made of Dawn,* won the Pulitzer Prize in 1969. His response is worth
repeating.
   "That is a very complicated subject, Joseph," he said. "As an uncle,
let me caution you. It is not easy to even talk about Indian humor."
   Advice such as that is not to be taken lightly. But, then again, neither is Native American humor. It is a truly serious subject. I've already
mentioned earlier in this book that Vine Deloria Jr. thought it important enough to devote an entire chapter of *Custer Died for Your Sins* to
"Indian Humor." *Custer Died for Your Sins,* which is subtitled *An Indian
Manifesto,* laid the groundwork for much of the Native American activism and political awareness which has taken place over the past two
decades. Deloria's book aimed at countering the many stereotypes about
the aboriginal people of North America. Few things rely more on stereotype than ethnic humor, so Deloria's decision to devote twenty pages
to a discussion of the way humor functions among American Indian
people was both an obvious choice and a bold one.
   In commenting on the prevalence of humor among American Indians, Deloria went so far as to say:

The Indian people are exactly opposite of the popular stereotype. I sometimes wonder how anything is accomplished by Indians because of the apparent overemphasis on humor within the Indian world. Indians have found a humorous side of nearly every problem and the experiences of life have generally been so well defined through jokes and stories that they have become a thing in themselves.[3]

Going even further, Deloria concludes that humor is not just present in contemporary American Indian life, it is integral to its existence:

Humor has come to occupy such a prominent place in national Indian affairs that any kind of movement is impossible without it. ... The more desperate the problem, the more often humor is directed to describe it.[4]

Much humor—whether American Indian or Jewish, Ghanaian or Irish, Melanesian or middle-class American—is only funny to those who are deeply connected to the culture from which that humor comes. Some things, too, don't work outside the context from which they originated. Puns and wordplay of all sorts—which are common throughout Native North America—are hard to translate out of their original languages. As Momaday pointed out to me later on in our discussion, he remembered very clearly some of the old Kiowa men telling jokes which would seem totally unfunny to anyone not Kiowa. In fact, some non-Indians might be totally puzzled by what passed for humor among them.

▲▼▲

Louis Oliver is a Creek Indian writer in his eighties whom I've mentioned several times. As an example of a joke which Creeks find hilariously funny but which non-Indians shake their heads in confusion about, he told me the following:

It was spring and the wild onions were up big enough to gather. Saturday and the Indians were in town to get supplies. One Indian stood on the street corner just looking at the traffic and passers-by. He had eaten a good dish of wild onions at home. A friend of his came up to him and noticed a piece of green onion on his teeth. So he said, "Are the onions up pretty good?" With a broad grin, the man who'd just eaten onions answered, "I don't know."

Louis went on to observe that it has been his experience in his long life that "Creek Indians cannot discuss any serious matters without allowing humor to intervene. It is known that in the old days in court sessions and trials, the questioning by lawyers and interpretations by interpreters brought on much roaring laughter."

▲▼▲

There is an Abenaki story which I've been told the old people thought very funny. There was a white trader who had a bad reputation. He was known for his temper and liked to cheat the Indians who came to trade with him. When they brought in their skins, he would pay for them by the pound, using an old-fashioned balance scale. However, instead of using a counterweight, he would place his hand in the tray and say, "My hand weighs just one pound." One day, the Indians had enough. They purchased a set of weights and went to the man's store to confront him as a cheat. The white trader, though, became angry, pulled out his gun and shot at them. The Indians shot back and killed the man. Then, just out of curiosity, they cut his hand off and put it on the scale, using their weights. They felt really bad when they discovered his hand weighed exactly one pound.

I have told that story to some non-Indians who've failed to see either the humor or the irony intended. It is as much a lesson story as a funny tale, and it cuts in a number of different ways. If you understand what makes people laugh, you are closer to understanding and appreciating those people themselves. If laughter is, as many have said, only the other side of tragedy, then learning something about the humor of a people also means learning something about their history. As in Louis Oliver's example of the Creek courtrooms, where the sense of humor of the plaintiffs and defendants had direct bearing on the outcome of their cases, humor can be an excellent way of making a point.

One famous anecdote about the Sioux Chief Spotted Tail tells how the U.S. government, after the discovery of gold, offered to lease the

Black Hills for a hundred years from the Indians, paying only a nominal rental. In the course of the discussion, Spotted Tail pointed to the mules owned by the government agents. "I like those mules," he said, "but I don't want to buy them. Can I just borrow them—for a hundred years?"

That story and another well known tale ascribed to a number of different Native Americans are clearly responses to the long history of dispossession of the Native American. The second story is one I first heard told about Red Jacket, the Seneca orator of the eighteenth century, but it has turned up among Indian people in the Midwest and the far West with one of their own people as the protagonist.

Red Jacket was out walking with a white friend who talked about the good treatment the Senecas enjoyed from their white neighbors. Red Jacket asked him to sit with him on a log near the river. But each time the man was comfortable, Red Jacket slid closer to him on the log and said, "Move over." Finally, the man was about to fall in the water. Red Jacket slid closer again. "Move over," he said. "But if I move further," the man said, "I'll fall in the water." "Yes," Red Jacket said, "and even so the whites tell us to move on when there is no place left to go."

A recent "Indian joke," which began making the rounds about the time when the race was on to send the first man to the moon, makes its point to those who are aware of the results of a U.S. government policy called "relocation." The idea was to relocate Indians from their reservations to big cities where they would quickly, the government felt, assimilate. The results were usually disastrous. The current problems of Indian alcoholism and joblessness in many urban centers were born, at least in part, out of relocation. A great many Indians, though, allowed themselves to be relocated and then, one way or another, made their way back to the rez. The joke went like this: The government has decided that the first man on the moon is going to be an Indian. How come? Because they can save money on an Indian. They're going to say that it's relocation. Then all they have to do is worry about getting him there. He'll find his own way home.

That same sort of humor is standard for the various Native American emcees who take over the microphones at powwows and other gatherings each summer to comment on the activities of the day and tell whatever Indian jokes they can think of that tie in to whatever is going on. Will Rogers, the Cherokee humorist and writer, seldom made remarks which emphasized his Indian identity. However, his famous columns clearly made use of both a very Indian dry sense of humor and that kind of topicality I hear every time I listen to a powwow emcee. Perhaps the best-known contemporary Indian humorist is an Oneida Indian named Charlie Hill, who has made a number of appearances on television. In an interview in the Native American magazine *Akwekon,* Hill pointed out his links with the powwow emcee tradition of stand-up comedy. He quoted Lenny Bruce's remark: "Satire is tragedy plus time," and made it clear that one of his objectives was to get people to "laugh with us and not at us." He noted that most white people seem to know the same five Indian jokes, all of which make use of insulting stereotypes. "But," he said, "as my Dad told me once, 'White people discovered everything except their own sense of humor.'"

▲▼▲

In Native American circles, humor is commonly used as a form of correction or a way of deflecting hostility into a lesson. When someone says, "that reminds me of a joke," you can bet money that their intention is not just to elicit a laugh but to make a point. I can remember times when I've been told jokes which were clearly meant to point out to me—gently, but clearly—that I had made a mistake.

I've often heard it said by Iroquois friends that it is good to sit in a circle because on the circle everyone is the same height. Humor can be used to remind people—who because of their achievements might be feeling a little too proud or important—that they are no more valuable than anyone else in the circle of life. Teasing someone who gets a little too "tall" may help them shrink back to the right height.

Teasing was "a method of control of social situations" as Deloria explained in his chapter "Indian Humor":

> Rather than embarrass members of the tribe publicly people used to tease individuals they considered out of step with the consensus of tribal opinion. In this way egos were preserved and disputes within the tribe of a personal nature were held to a minimum.
>
> Gradually people learned to anticipate teasing and began to tease themselves as a means of showing humility and at the same time advocating a course of action they deeply believed in. Men

would depreciate their feats to show they were not trying to run roughshod over tribal desires.[5]

Teasing works in many ways in Native American culture. I recently received a newsletter from an American Indian program at a major university. It contains photos of their first annual graduate honors banquet. The caption of one not only lists the three people but also indicates in parentheses that the man in the center, a very well known Iroquois artist, is "eyeing the ice cream." That kind of gentle teasing, in this case, makes it clear to an Indian reader how much that artist is liked and respected.

Teasing can have its rules, though. In certain Native American cultures there are people you are not allowed to tease. Elders, perhaps, were not to be teased by the very young. In many American Indian nations it was forbidden for a man to tease his mother-in-law and vice versa. I know of a young Native American man who used to go over to the house of one of the women of his mother's generation. They had become great friends, and he loved to sit by her pot-bellied stove and joke with her. She, in turn, would tease right back. He spent so much time at the woman's house that he got to know her daughter, an attractive young woman about his own age. A romance developed, and, finally, the two young people decided to marry. They had not been married long, though, before the young man became unhappy. His old friend was now his mother-in-law and he wasn't allowed to tease her. Their conversation with each other had to observe certain formalities. The new mother-in-law was also miserable. She missed those times when they'd sit around joking with each other. Finally, the daughter could stand it no longer because both her husband *and* her mother were impossible to live with now. She suggested they should divorce. Less than a month after the divorce was finalized, that young man was back sitting by the stove, teasing with his former mother-in-law.

Among the Iroquois, the strike-pole dance afforded an opportunity for clansmen to tell jokes on each other. These jokes might satirize the person's hunting ability or exaggerate some physical characteristic. A man would rise, strike the pole and then relate a story about one of his clan brothers. When he finished and everyone was done laughing, the joker would then give a small present to the butt of the joke to soothe any bad feelings. However, as the dance went on, you can be sure that the next person to strike the pole would be that same clan brother ready to outdo the joker in telling a story about him! It was a kind of humor which incorporated teasing with the kind of open participation which characterizes many other aspects of Indian life. Joking, like dancing, was something everyone did. Some years ago, someone said to an Apache friend of mine that they had heard that Jonathan Winters was Indian, and they knew about Will Rogers, but they wondered why there weren't more Indian comedians. His answer, which I'm not sure they understood, was simple—because there aren't more Indians. I guess he felt that 1.5 million (the 1980 census of Native Americans) was a sufficient number.

▲▼▲

The place of sacred clowns in Native American cultures has sometimes been observed. These clowns and masked dancers often are closely connected to healing and to the most awesome powers of the universe, even though their antics are the source of a great deal of laughter—as anyone can attest who has ever seen, for example, the arrival of the clowns during the Hopi *katsina* dances. Emory Sekaquaptewa's wonderful article "One More Smile for a Hopi Clown" points out that "the heart of the Hopi concept of clowning is that we are all clowns." By being compared to clowns "we know that this is to be a trying life and that we will try to fulfill our destiny by mimicry, by mockery, by copying, whatever."[6] The role of the clown is not to take one's mind off their troubles, but to point out ways we can survive and even laugh. He tells how one man who was very devoted to his sacred clowning began to think in his old age of ways he could be remembered as a clown. His solution was to leave a last request, which was fulfilled after his death. His nephews and sons dressed him in his clown costume and carried him to a rooftop. The town crier assembled all the people and then, after swinging the man's body between them four times as they called out *Yaahahay,* they threw his corpse down, plop, into the plaza, laughing as they did so. The people were surprised, but they laughed, too.

Among the Iroquois, the sacred beings who have been called "false faces" (though I dislike the implications of that word "false") appear at certain times of the year. They behave like children, begging for food, rolling on the floors and talking strangely. Their behavior is amusing, but they are also very powerful. They go to the woodstove and pull out the embers, juggling them in bare hands without being burned. Then they rub the ashes from the fire onto the heads of those who are sick and wish to be healed. Similar amusing antics on the part of other Native American clownlike beings and similar reverence blended with laughter on the part of those who observe can be seen throughout North American Indian cultures. The Indian clown might be seen as a combination of Eddie Murphy and Pope John Paul. This sort of blending of so-called "sacred" and "profane" behaviors accounts for one of the differences between European humor and American Indian humor. In writing of the Navajo, W. W. Hill noted:

> The greatest contrast between Navaho and European humor lies in the degree of participation. Navaho culture possesses no system of social stratification, and because of this it is possible for every individual in the culture to participate wholly in all aspects of humorous expression. In our culture, social and educational status determine to a large extent our type of humor.[7]

Washington Matthews, an ethnologist who was noted for his studies of Navajo life, describes one sacred clown in *The Night Chant: A Navajo Ceremony*. Water Sprinkler, the god of rain, is impersonated by a clown who constantly misses cues in the dancing, drops important items and is generally confused. Other southwestern peoples have clowns in their sacred ceremonies who engage in mock copulation with each other, pick up feces and behave in ways which a Western observer might consider far removed from the sacred—unless that observer was aware of ancient European ceremonies in which sacred clowns played a vital part. Some of those traditions still existed strongly in the Christian churches of the Middle Ages. There the ridiculous and the sublime were freely mixed at certain times of the year, such as December 28 and the Festival of the Innocents which James Frazer describes in *The Golden Bough*.

Hundreds of extremely different Native peoples and languages existed in pre-Columbian North America, and that diversity of the Native American peoples has seldom been clearly expressed by those who have portrayed the "Indian" in print or in film. There are, however, some things which seem to have been true of American Indians throughout the continent in the past and which remain true to this day. One of those things, which binds Indian people together in a loose union, is the complex phenomena which might be called "Indian humor." Wherever you go in "Indian Country," you will find laughter—a laughter which may be bawdy one minute, sacred the next. But whichever it is, you can be sure that it is a humor which makes its point clear to Native Americans, and that point includes the importance of humility and the lesson that laughter leads to learning and survival.

Notes

1. Arthur Parker, *The Indian How Book* (Mineola, NY: Dover Publications, 1975).
2. Richard I. Dodge, *Our Wild Indians—Thirty-three Years' Personal Experience among the Red Men of the Great West* (North Stratford, NH: Ayer Company Publishers, repr. of 1883 ed.).
3. Vine Deloria Jr., *Custer Died for Your Sins: An Indian Manifesto* (New York: Macmillan, 1969).
4. Ibid.
5. Ibid.
6. Emory Sekaquaptewa, "One More Smile for a Hopi Clown," in *The South Corner of Time,* ed. Larry Evers (Tucson: Sun Tracks, 1980).
7. W. W. Hill, "Navajo Humor," *General Studies in Anthropology,* No. 9 (Menahsa, WI: George Banta, 1943).

The Way a Medicine Person Sees the World

✡

Advice

There was a man
who was feeling troubled.

He went to see an analyst.
The office was filled with brilliant light,
so bright that when he tried to read
the diplomas covering the walls,
all he could make out was a blur of letters
and the hazy reflection of his own face.

The doctor waited behind his desk.
Sit down, he said.
The man sat down.

I'm worried, the man said, *about my job.*
I have to work hard and the hours are long.
I'm afraid the people I work with don't like me.

Quit your job, said the doctor,
If you don't have a job,
then you won't have to work.

I'm worried, the man said, *about my family.*
I'm afraid they'll be hurt and when I travel
I don't like to leave them behind.

If I were you, the doctor said,
I'd cook my family and eat them.
Then nothing would ever hurt them again
and they would always be with you.

The man was confused, but he kept on talking.
I'm worried, he said, *about people dying.*
Why is there such a thing as death?

One day Creator and Coyote
walked together beside the big river.
No one had died yet and Creator
threw a piece of wood into the stream.
If this floats, he said,
everyone will live forever.

Sure enough, the wood floated,
but then Coyote picked up a stone.
Let me try that, he said.

The man looked closer at the doctor
and said, *Why do you have such big teeth?*

All the better to chew up facts,
the doctor said with a toothy grin.

And why do you have such great big ears?

All the better to hear
all the gossip I spread.

And why do you have such a long bushy tail?

All the better to trip over it
when I think too much
of my own advice.

Then the doctor stood up
and tripped over his tail.
He rolled around and around
on the floor and the man laughed,
the man laughed and laughed.

He fell on the floor, too,
and forgot all his troubles.

And when he stopped laughing,
Coyote was gone.

Few writers in the last three decades have been the subject of more controversy and interest than Carlos Castaneda. The publication of the first of his *Don Juan* books led to a long debate involving anthropologists, literary critics and latter-day mystics as they searched for the truth and fiction in his writing. As I indicated in an earlier essay, the general consensus now seems to be that Don Juan never existed and that Castaneda, like Coyote, is a Trickster. Both "truth" and "fiction" can be relative terms. I'm not about to discuss how much of Castaneda's epic came out of his own life experiences and how much was borrowed from articles written by other anthropologists such as Peter Furst. Furst is well known in ethnological circles for his studies of the uses of mind-altering substances among Meso-American peoples and for his description of a Mexican Indian shaman's balancing exploits on top of a waterfall, published a year before Castaneda's second book in which Don Genaro does much the same feat. I'd like, instead, to say a bit about the way some Native American people have told me they viewed the Castaneda books and what their views say about that world of the sacred, which Castaneda originally intended to encounter (he says) as a somewhat detached anthropological observer.

Anthropologists have long been viewed with suspicion by Native American people. All too often, these men and women, with strange costumes and outlandish customs, have intruded upon peaceful villages, loaded down with notebooks, recording devices and cameras, asking impolite questions they would never ask of any of their non-Native friends and acting superior. They seem to have forgotten, if they ever knew, that Native American people have been studying the "European" for more than four hundred years. Squanto, for example, whose invaluable assistance enabled the Plymouth colonists to survive the long, bitter winter of 1681–1682, had lived in Europe where he had been taken as a slave before the Pilgrims' arrival. He spoke the English language and had managed to return home only a short time before the Pilgrims arrived. As Vine Deloria pointed out in *Custer Died for Your Sins,* Native American people often understood the whites better than the whites understood themselves. Whatever an anthropologist writes about a particular Native American people finds its way into their hands in record time.

For a long time there has been a sort of game in Indian Country called "putting on the anthros." (There is even a song recorded by Sioux singer Floyd Westerman with the lines, "Here come the anthros, better hide your past away.") Whenever an anthropologist asks questions in certain Native American communities, he can always count on answers, but they are often not the ones he wanted to get. In James Mooney's writings about the sacred formulas of the Cherokees, all of his "informants" were careful to never give him the right words and ingredients for their incantations. Wherever Mooney has the color black, for example, you can bet that the real color was white or blue or red. Once, an anthropologist collecting stories at a certain pueblo in the Southwest took almost a week to realize that the story they were telling him about their origins, which included an extremely dense character who was always making mistakes, was being made up on the spot and he was that character! If, in fact, the whole Don Juan saga which Castaneda has been chronicling for more than two decades has been fabricated and is nothing more than a series of very imaginative novels (for which Castaneda was awarded both a master's degree and a Ph.D.—in anthropology, not creative writing—from the University of California at Berkeley), then we might say that he is working within a rather well established Native American tradition.

I have always felt that one of the major selling points for the Castaneda books (and the many imitators of Castaneda who have become popular in the decades since *The Teachings of Don Juan*) is the stance of disbeliever who only reluctantly becomes convinced of the magical truth he is being offered. After being shown all kinds of paranormal wonders, after a hundred visionary experiences, even after being initiated as a wizard and performing magical feats himself, Carlos remains the quintessential westerner, the disbeliever, the man from Missouri who always says, "Show me!" He does such a good job at being a skeptic that he convinces his readers of the reality of the fantastic events all around him, which he is too thick to see. His readers love that—his

Western readers, that is. But what about the Native Americans who read, for example, *The Teachings of Don Juan?*

In 1973 I had a conversation with Leslie Silko, the MacArthur Fellowship winning poet, novelist and movie maker from Laguna Pueblo. Leslie told me that she had recently spoken to some of her Native American students in a class she was teaching about Castaneda's book. She read them the section in which Don Juan turns Carlos into a crow. The class ended and the students went home. The next day, though, when they came in, some of them had dreamy looks in their eyes. "What's up?" she asked. They smiled at each other, and finally one of them answered. "I tried that turning into a crow last night. It wasn't that hard. Then I spent the night flying over the valley." To them, it seemed, the reality of Don Juan was not a strange one at all. Taking part in that reality was, to them, a logical response. I do not mean that they went out and picked peyote and ate it. That *was* the response of hundreds, even thousands, of non-Indians who read Castaneda. In fact, it resulted in the near extermination of the peyote cactus from many parts of California and northern Mexico. Native American people such as the Huichol gather the peyote in a careful, limited and sacramental fashion. They do so to ensure that this very slow-growing plant will not be wiped out. Peyote is an important healing plant for many Native American people, and its destruction is a tragedy. It may have been with that in mind, aware that a generation of young Anglo truth seekers were decimating the plant, that Castaneda reports in his third book that the use of peyote or any drugs at all is not just unnecessary but a hindrance to the work of the sorcerer.

"We take," a Nez Perce writer named Phil George said to me, "that world which Castaneda got so excited about for granted." He paused for a moment. "But taking it for granted doesn't mean that we do not respect it." Another friend, Peter Blue Cloud, the Mohawk writer, just laughed and said, "Hell, my aunt does better than Don Juan any day of the week." He chuckled, too, over *Rolling Thunder* by Douglas Boyd, a book which tells about a contemporary Cherokee shaman. "Man," he said, "did old Rolling Thunder have fun with that guy Boyd!" He didn't mean that Rolling Thunder was a faker as a medicine person, only that many of the miraculous events which Boyd witnessed were jokes being played on him in a good-natured way.

Blue Cloud laughed. "You know," he said, "one time old Rolling Thunder was visiting the [Akwesasne] *Notes* offices. Me and my friend, he always called us 'those wild Indians,' were sitting up top of the stairs behind the door when we heard him coming up. 'Where are those wild Indians?' he said. Then, when he got to the top of the stairs, and we said Hi! to him from behind the door, he jumped a mile! 'Why'd you scare me like that?' he said. 'Heck, you're the medicine man,' we said. 'Couldn't you see us there behind that door?'"

Standing Deer, an Indian activist who is still serving time in the Marion Federal Prison, once wrote me a letter that made reference to Castaneda. He told me about his grandmother who spoke only her Native tongue to him when he was a child living in a remote section of McCurtin County, Oklahoma. "Grandmother would say something like 'Day after tomorrow at sunset so-and-so and his wife and three of the children will be here with us. The oldest boy will stay at home because he is sick.' Nobody said, 'Wow! How do you know that? ... except me. She would tell me that last night she soared on the wings of an Eagle and saw them leaving their digs (which was a two and one-half day trip to where we hung out). I was the anthro and she was Rolling Thunder." Standing Deer went on to say, "I guess I amaze easily, but I have always been amazed at the way linear-thinking folks like anthros arrive at 'truth' according to whether things 'really' happened or if they were dreams or imaginings. I have never been all that good at distinguishing 'dreams' from 'reality.' I have always had the notion that if it happens within the awareness of a human mammal or any of our relations—then it happened."

There has been, as I've written elsewhere, a long tradition of turning to the Indian people of this continent for wisdom and enlightenment. It is not a bad idea, for there is still much real wisdom held by Native American people, the kind of wisdom we, as human beings, can either live by or die for the lack of. But there is also—and Indian people are very aware of this—the possibility that their wisdom will, once again, be misunderstood or exploited. I have been told by some Native American medicine people that they know cures for certain kinds of cancer. I believe them—and isn't it true that aspirin simply came from the same willow bark Native people used for thousands of years to cure headaches and that quinine is made from the bark of a South American tree which many Native people, there, used for malaria? There are many other remedies which were originated by American Indian healers that are now in use as patented pharmaceuticals. So why haven't their cures for cancer been given to the world? Perhaps it is because the time is not right, or because certain medicines only work when they are properly used, and the proper use may include the right spiritual relationship between healer and patient.

A young Indian man I knew had been going out a lot with his non-Indian friends, a college crowd that drank a lot and smoked a good deal of marijuana. He was losing touch with his family. Finally, one evening just before the son was about to go out, his father took him aside. "Come here," he said, "let's smoke together." Then the father brought out some tobacco. Before they smoked, however, he blessed it with corn pollen and spoke a prayer. This time when the young man smoked, he saw things he had never seen before when he was smoking marijuana, visions so beautiful and true that he began to cry. The world was in balance for him in a way it had never been before.

"What do you see?" his father asked.

The young man told him. "I don't understand," the son said, "pot never made me see the world like this."

"It wasn't what we smoked," his father said. "You're just seeing now through your own eyes."

Then the son asked the question the father had been waiting to hear. "Is this how a medicine man sees the world?"

"Yes," his father answered, "this is the way a medicine person sees the world all of the time."

PART IV

GATHERING THE BONES

Red Hand

(A Seneca Story)

Long ago, there was a man named Red Hand, who was a good hunter. Not only was he usually successful when he went to hunt, he also showed great respect for the animals and birds. Before he hunted he would always throw tobacco and ask permission to hunt for game. He would never kill a mother animal with young. He did not take unfair advantage by shooting animals when they were swimming or asleep, and he never hunted unless he and the other people of his village were in need. Whenever he was successful, he would share part of his kill, calling to the birds of the air and the animals such as the wolf and the fox to come share. When he harvested his fields, he always left some of the ears of corn on the ground and called to the crows and other birds to come and take their part. Because of this, he was loved by all of the animals and birds.

One day, he went with a party of other men on a journey to the south to trade with another nation. As they traveled through the forest, they were ambushed by a party of men from another nation with whom they had been at war. In the fight, Red Hand was separated from the others and struck down by a war club. Then, as he lay there, the enemies cut his scalp from his head and took it back to their village as a trophy.

After a time, night came and the owl, seeing the man lying there, came and hovered above his body. A wolf caught the scent of the man's blood and came close. When he saw the man's face, he recognized him as the great friend of the animals, and he sat beside his body and howled in sorrow. Before long, all of the birds and animals who had been treated with respect and fed by Red Hand had gathered.

The great eagle perched on a stump above the man's body. "This is our friend," said the eagle. "What shall we do?"

"He is the one who feeds us," said the wolf. "We must not let him die."

"If he grows too cold, he cannot return to life again. I will keep the warmth in him," said the bear. Then it lifted up Red Hand's body and held it close.

"A human being cannot live without his scalp," said the owl. "It must be restored to him."

Then the crow flew through the forest until it came to the village where the enemy people lived. The crow saw the scalp, hanging from a pole near the smoke hole of a lodge, but when it flew too close, the people threw rocks at it to chase it away. When the crow returned, it told what it had seen.

"I will go and bring back our brother's scalp," said the heron. It, too, flew to the village of the enemy people, but it, too, was driven away.

Next to try was the falcon. It was swifter than the others, but when it swooped in to grasp the scalp, the enemy people saw it and fired arrows so close that it barely escaped with its life.

Then the little hummingbird flew off. It was so small and swift it could hardly be seen. It dove down and speared the scalp with its sharp beak and flew swiftly back to where the animals waited in the clearing.

The great eagle took the dry scalp and shook the dew from its wings onto it, moistening it again.

"Now we must make a powerful medicine," the eagle said.

Then each of the birds and animals gathered there gave a part of their own flesh to mix with herbs and clear water from a nearby spring into a powerful medicine. They poured it into Red Hand's mouth and pressed the moist scalp onto his head. As soon as they did so, Red Hand began to breathe deeply. He heard the sounds of the animals around him, and he could understand their voices. He opened his eyes and there, all around him in the moonlight, he saw the animals who had healed him.

Then, as he sat there, the animals explained what they had done. They told him how to make that healing medicine, which would be the most powerful medicine the Seneca people would ever know.

"You have been our greatest friend. So we give you this medicine," they told him. "Take it back to your people."

So, from that day on, Red Hand was a great healer. The medicine he was given was able to heal all wounds. It became known as the *niga'ni'ga'a,* the "Little Water Medicine." It was passed down within the Medicine Lodge from generation to generation. Those who were to be entrusted with it always had to show their gratitude through songs and dances to the medicine animals. That way the people would always remember to be thankful to the birds and animals who saved the life of their greatest friend.

Waking Up to the Seven Directions

Many of us walk through our lives as if we are sleeping. The American existential philosopher, Henry David Thoreau, whose view of life was more deeply affected by American Indians than most people know, said that he had never met a man who was completely awake. (Thoreau's last words were "moose" and "Indian" and he had been planning to write a major book about the American Indian before his death in 1862.)

It is also said in many traditional American Indian stories that human beings are the weakest of all the beings in creation. Our eyes are weaker than those of the hawk. Our hearing is much less keen than that of the deer. Our noses cannot match that of the wolf.

There are ways, though, to become stronger and more fully awake. We can learn from the birds and animals—those wiser beings Tom Porter, a Mohawk elder, describes as our teachers. While we human beings forget the most basic things, such as caring for our own children, the birds and animals do not forget. We must look to them to help us remember, to wake us up again to the world around us and within us. Watch how the birds—both the mother and father—feed their little ones, giving up their own food to make the next generation strong. See how all of the wolves in a pack, not just the parents, but all of the adults, watch over and care for the cubs.

To learn, we must once again open our eyes and our ears. I was given a wampum belt by my sister, Margaret. When I look at it, it helps me remember many things. That wampum belt bears on it the designs which hold some of the most ancient Wabanaki teachings. In the center is a white cross. That stands for the creation of the one called Gluskabe, whose name might be translated as the "Storyteller" or the "Talking Person." His head toward *Pebonki,* the "Winterland," his feet toward *Sawanki,* the "Summerland," one arm toward the sunrise, one arm toward the sunset, he was created on Earth, created from Earth.

Two crosses with hollow centers stand to each side of that central white cross. Those four crosses are the four directions, each direction alive with the breath of life, each direction the source of a living wind. Those winds entered into the body of the one called Gluskabe. Those winds gave him life just as the winds of breath give life to us all. The Dineh people of the Southwest say that the swirls on our hands and feet, our fingers and toes, are the marks of those winds of breath which give life.

To either side of those five crosses are seven jagged lines marked in white. Those lines stand for the seven grandmothers and seven grandfathers who are the ancestors of all human beings. They also stand for the seven sacred directions—*Kik ta Spemkik,* "Earth and Sky," the Four Cardinal Directions and the place between all those, the Seventh Direction, which has been described as the spiritual knowledge of life held in each person's heart. It may be said that each of us is the Seventh Direction, for we all walk between Earth and Sky, between Sunrise and Sunset, between Winterland and Summerland. But if we do not look into our hearts, we do not know where we are. If we do not look into our hearts, we never realize that the sacred is within us and we do not know who we are.

Seven also stands for the openings in our heads. When Gluskabe was created, his head was closed. He could see and hear and sense nothing. Ktsi Nwaskw, the "Great Mystery," made the lightning strike seven times. The first double strike of lightning made two ears. Thus, Gluskabe could hear both sides. The second double strike made two eyes. Thus, Gluskabe could see the near and the far, see the world in depth. The third double strike made two nostrils. Thus, Gluskabe could smell that which was sweet and that which was sour. The last, seventh single strike of lightning made one mouth. Only one mouth was needed, for all of us like Gluskabe, should speak only half as much as we listen, half as much as we observe, half as much as we smell the world around us.

Listen, listen, listen, listen.

The river's flow
follows the voice of the land.
Snow melts
from a cupped hand.

Are you ready to hear
the voice of the rain?

GATHERING THE BONES

✸

There is an old story among the Abenaki peoples. *Let the bones come together now.* The hero has reached the place where his enemies are strongest. It may be a forsaken valley or an island in the middle of an enchanted lake. Let us call this hero Bedegwadzo, "Big Mountain," for that is one name by which such a hero in the old tales is still called by the Abenaki people of northeastern Vermont. Bedegwadzo looks around. There are bones all around. They are the bones of others who came to this place. They came seeking tobacco, perhaps. Or perhaps they were trapped by the ones who have great magical power, the ones who can fly through the air faster than birds, who can lift great stones as if they were pebbles, who speak words unlike those used by ordinary human beings. The ones who died here were young and strong, unafraid of the great odds against them. Their weapons, though, were not those of the sorcerers, their own magic not as strong as that of the ones who knew the secrets of power. They have died. Only their bones are left, and the bones are scattered. Bedegwadzo stands there for a long time, saying nothing, looking around. Then he begins to gather the bones. He puts them back together. He shouts at the top of his voice, "LET THE BONES COME TOGETHER! MY PEOPLE, GET UP! YOUR ENEMY IS RETURNING!!"

Then the bones stand up, and they are alive again. The people who died, who were gone forever—or so everyone assumed—return to life. Some of them laugh. Some cry. Others cannot believe that they are alive. A few, in their haste to come back, have gotten the wrong bones. There is one man with a leg that is too short, another with an arm that is too long. That, the story tells us, is why there are cripples today. But they are alive. And Bedegwadzo sends them back home.

▲▼▲

America is a land made of myths. One of those myths is that the Indians were ignorant and savage. Yet one of the men who met the Pilgrims, who showed them how to grow food, who saved that pathetic gathering of refugees, was not only a man of great humanity and intelligence but had traveled farther in his life than any of the Pilgrims. He already spoke English, for this Indian man, Squanto by name, who met them in Plymouth in 1620, had been to England—taken as a slave and later freed. Despite that slavery, despite the rapid spread of European diseases (measles, smallpox, whooping cough, syphilis) brought by European fishermen and traders (diseases which decimated the population of the Northeast, leaving great areas of land open for the incoming Europeans, land which had already been cleared and turned into productive agricultural land by the Indians), he and others of the people of the Atlantic Coast tried to welcome the Pilgrims. They allowed them the use of land kept cleared by the Native people, which now lay fallow because so many people had died from the plagues brought by the ships from Europe. It was not virgin land which the Pilgrims settled on, it was land which had been widowed.

For a long time, the Wampanoags and the other people of the coast tried to live in peace with the newcomers. It was only after many betrayals on the part of those paler-skinned immigrants that the wars began, wars which continue today in other forms, for many Indian nations never surrendered or were finally beaten. Some, like the Abenaki, just disappeared. And that is another myth. The myth of the extinction of the Native American. Today, perhaps, people are more ready to believe that Indians were not completely wiped out in North America. They accept that there are "real Indians" west of the Mississippi. But the ones in the East? Conventional wisdom says they are all gone, or most of them, or that the few left are acculturated or their blood so thinned by intermarriage with non-Indians that they are not Indians at all. They have never heard the story of how Bedegwadzo gathered together the bones.

▲▼▲

Perhaps at this point someone may be thinking, who cares about a few thousand Indians. Let me explain why, aside from my own ties of blood, these things concern me and concern us all. We, too, stand close to that valley of bones. All of us, not just the Indian people. There are no tombstones to mark the dead in that valley, only that ludicrously familiar mushroom cloud. (I write this only a few days after the anniversaries of Hiroshima and Nagasaki, and the voice of a local congressman praising the bomb for saving so many lives that would have been lost in an invasion of Japan was loud on the radio and TV channels.) You might say, too, that America is at the edge of a familiar forest. It is the same deep forest the early pioneers such as Daniel Boone loved and feared, longed for and then destroyed. Step a short distance into the trees and you are again in hostile lands. Like Vietnam in the 1960s, Central America is only a step beyond the gold rush and the wagon trains. Or the Middle East, or Chernobyl or the bombing of the federal office building in Oklahoma City. There is no end to the list of possible human-made disasters—and I have yet to mention what we have done to the air and the water and the earth, to the fragile ecosystems that sustain life on this planet. If we can learn from our past—and from the present—if we see clearly what has happened, what is still happening, what may happen again, we may not fall over that edge. Some say there is no way of stopping it. The past, they say, is dead. But when we see a people who were forgotten, scorned, written off—yet who continued to survive—we may believe, instead, that there is still hope, that the bones may come together again.

▲▼▲

The Abenaki were among the first. *Abenaki.* The "People of the Dawn Land." That is what the word means, and if you look to the northeast corner of this continent, on the Great Turtle's back, your eyes will be turned toward their traditional lands, the places where they lived, where they continue to live. There, where the sun's rays first strike North America, the Abenaki people have lived for thousands of years. The Abenaki people include the Western Abenaki (whose lands include New Hampshire, Vermont, parts of northern New York and Canada) and the Eastern Abenaki (predominantly, the Penobscot, whose lands include much of western and central Maine). The larger term *Wabanaki* also includes the related nations of Passamaquoddy in eastern Maine and the Malisett and Micmac people of New Brunswick and Nova Scotia. According to most modern reckonings (which are constantly being revised upward), the populations today of Wabanaki people total well over twenty thousand. There are ten thousand Micmacs alone. The population of Penobscots, who, with the Passamaquoddys, won the largest land claims case in history against the federal government in 1980, number about two thousand. The Passamaquoddy themselves are about twenty-five hundred. The Missisquoi Abenaki in the United States (Vermont, in particular) and Canada stand at perhaps two thousand, and the Abenaki of Canada, most of whom are connected to the Odanak reserve north of Montreal, are numbered in the region of at least one thousand. Considering history, it is amazing that there are any Abenakis left at all!

▲▼▲

According to the records in history books, the Abenaki were among the first Native peoples of North America to encounter Europeans. Giovanni da Verrazano sailed the coast of Maine in 1524. He described the Abenakis as people who already had some experience dealing with Europeans and were wary of them, refusing to allow Verrazano's men to land on shore. Considering the fact that the usual pattern of Europeans (including Columbus) in the New World was to be warmly greeted by the Native people and then proceed to clap those same "Indians" in irons to take them back to Europe as slaves, one has to admit that the Abenakis had a good idea of who they were dealing with! As a result, Verrazano called them "bad people." It is a label which the Abenaki have been given often throughout their long history of understanding and dealing with the whites.

If one looks at certain Abenaki oral traditions, it appears that dealing with Europeans, or at least some knowledge of their existence, goes far back beyond Verrazano or Columbus. It is my own opinion that Norse ships made their way to the North American continent and the lands of the Abenaki and their northern Algonquin cousins at least five centuries before Columbus. But those Norse colonies were abandoned, wiped out or absorbed. Perhaps it may explain why there are similarities between certain Norse folk stories and some Abenaki traditions, and why as early as the late 1500s, Europeans remarked upon the fact that a great many of the Native people of New England had green eyes. As has been true in other parts of North America—South Dakota, for example, where the influx of French Canadian traders marrying Lakota women in the 1700s and 1800s has resulted in French surnames being extremely common among modern-day Lakotas—the influence of the Europeans has been only skin deep. Though European names, technology and genes spread among the Native people, the traditional cultures have been strong enough to survive in spite of it all.

▲▼▲

Early on during the European invasion of *Ndakinna* ("Our Land"), the Abenaki allied themselves with the French. For a time, the Abenaki people remained as neutral as possible, but the waves of plagues which swept over their lands made it hard for them to maintain control of their own lands and destinies against the onrush of the English from the southeast. The diseases of Europe—smallpox, plague, syphilis, influenza, measles, whooping cough and many others—were not found in North America prior to the fifteenth century. There was no resistance to them. Between 1616 and 1619 smallpox raged through the Abenaki Nations. Between the coast of Maine and the shores of Lake Champlain, there had been at least thirty thousand Abenakis, probably more. At least 50 percent of the Abenaki people may have died in that epidemic. Similar losses occurred in the epidemics of 1633 and 1639. One writer about the Abenaki, Colin Calloway, estimates that of the ten thousand or so Western Abenaki, only five hundred survived by the end of the seventeenth century. The only modern comparisons, in which 95 percent of the people are wiped out, might be an unchecked epidemic of AIDS or a global nuclear war.

It was to the Abenaki that the French brought Christianity, the British a policy of offering a bounty of one hundred pounds for a single Abenaki scalp. That difference in policy toward the Abenaki was the reason for the massacre which took place at Norrigwock on August 24, 1724. In that massacre Father Sebastian Rasles, the French priest to the Abenaki, was killed. William Carlos Williams wrote about Father Rasles in his book *In the American Grain*. Rasles put together a dictionary of the Abenaki language. He listened to the Abenaki. He tried to help them keep their land against the British. Though the motives of the French were, perhaps, no nobler than those of the British in seeking control of the New World, its wealth and furs, the French sought it in a different way. The idea of the French was to control North America through their Indian allies. Few French settled in North America to stay. The French were probably better allies than the English—who introduced the practice of widespread scalping bounties (scalping, it appears, was either nonexistent or rare before 1500 among Native Americans)—during the so-called French and Indian Wars, which were a North American continuance of the hundred-year struggle between the English and the French. In 1755, on the third day of November, the Massachusetts House of Representatives in Boston proclaimed a bounty on Penobscot Indian scalps as follows: "For every scalp of a male Indian brought in as evidence of their being killed as aforesaid, forty pounds. For every scalp of such female Indian or male Indian under the age of twelve years ... twenty pounds." There was, it appears, originally no word in Abenaki for scalping. One had to be invented—*Kinjamus,* an adaptation from the words "King James."

The French, too, came in smaller numbers. Their interests were (not necessarily in this order) to save heathen souls and to make money through trade. The British, on the other hand, had little interest in saving Indian souls. They were interested in clearing the land—but not of trees. The Indians of New England had been preparing those fields for thousands of years, clearing them for the traditional crops of corn, beans and squash: the Three Sisters. Instead, the British wished to clear the land of the Indians themselves—by purchase if possible—though the Native people had no concept of selling land, only of leasing it for the lessee's lifetime and in a manner which did not exclude (the Indians thought) continued Indian use of that land. The British also tried, though not so successfully, to take the land by force of arms. The Native people were expert guerrilla fighters, and few Indian wars were totally successful unless the whites had one or more allies. Their best allies were other Indian nations (the British pitting the Iroquois against the Abenaki) and European diseases. Especially diseases. By the early 1700s it was common practice to send women infected with venereal disease among the Indians and to give blankets from victims of smallpox to the Native people. They also introduced alcohol, which still takes its toll on Native nations to this day. It is only in the last few years (in large part through the efforts of Michael Dorris and Louise Erdrich, two contemporary Native American writers who live in New England) that the public has begun to be aware of the effect of alcohol on Native American children whose mothers drink heavily, resulting in fetal alcohol syndrome. (The incidence of FAS appears to be highest in the world among Native Americans and Russians.)

As they accepted the French as allies, the Abenaki also accepted their Christian religion and their names. The majority of Wabanaki today are Roman Catholic—though many aspects of traditional pre-Christian ways and spiritual practices continue. Just how deep, how widespread, those old ways remain is a subject I cannot and should not discuss. But there are other places in the world—Africa and the West Indies, for example—where Native people have successfully blended traditional religious practices with an understanding of what it is to be a "good Catholic." N. Scott Momaday's powerful novel of the Jemez Pueblo people of the American Southwest, *House Made of Dawn,* offers a very accurate picture of such syncretism. So it is that among today's Western Abenaki people we find last names such as St. Francis and Sabattis (St. John Baptiste) and also such older names as Obomsawin ("Keeper of the Council Fire"). The present-day chief of the Vermont Abenaki is a St. Francis. The chief at Odanak in Canada is an Obomsawin. (Alanis Obomsawin, who also hails from Odanak, is a contemporary writer and filmmaker. Her films have been supported and honored by the Canadian Film Board, and her writings have appeared in numerous publications, including *First People, First Voices,* an anthology of Canadian Indian writing from the University of Toronto Press.)

The British, though, sought to control the land by driving out both the Indians and the French. That raid on Norrigwock, which was intended to kill Rasles, was not the first. The British had tried before. They had burned both the village of Norrigwock and the chapel in the winter of 1705. This time they succeeded. In that same raid, Bomazeen, one of the great chiefs, a leader of the Kennebec Abenaki, was surprised en route and killed. Surrounded by the whites and their guns, he held a cross in his right hand and sang a death song as the muskets sounded.

Bomazeen. The name comes from *Obum-sawin.* It means "Keepers of the Ceremonial Fire." It is a name which has been spelled many ways by Abenaki people, some of whom still carry variations of that name. Joseph Obowmasawine was a veteran of the War of 1812, fighting on the Canadian side. Today, at Odanak (the Abenaki reserve on the St. Francis River in Quebec Province), the Obomsawin family still lives. And the name Cowin, which was that of a family of Indians in Vermont in the late 1800s, probably came from Obomsawin. Names are changed frequently from father to son among the Abenaki. Sometimes an Abenaki name has been Gallicized, then re-Abenaki-ized, then An-glicized. Sabbatist. Saint Jean-Baptiste. Sabbatis. St. Pierre. Sa Bial. Sabael. Obum-sawin. Bomazeen. Bowman. The name of my mother's father—Jesse Bowman. It is confusing to non-Indians, confusing to historians and ethnologists. And though such confusion may not have been the purpose of the continual change of names—for example, the son of Simon Obomsowin calling himself William Simon—the Abenaki are not displeased by it. Their history for the last hundred years and more has been that of a people who have survived their deaths by dying, survived their disappearance by disappearing, remained by going away while never leaving.

Somewhere, in the northern waters of Lake Champlain, there is a small island made of stone. On the maps it is called by a European name. I will not mention that name here or its location, for that island, which is sometimes called by its Abenaki name of Wo-ja-ho-sen, has been visited often in recent years by non-Indians who are fascinated by "places of power." They do not come to leave gifts to tobacco, as the old people did whenever they passed this place on their way across the lake. They bring with them chisels and hammers, and they break away pieces of that stone to take with them as souvenirs.

There are other places in the world where those who visit places of power try to take away some of the magic with them—not in their hearts and memories, but in their pockets and purses. I was talking not long ago with a friend who is a ranger in Volcano National Park on the Big Island of Hawaii. There are special places on Hawaii where stones have been placed in certain ways on the earth, stones which are easy to pick up and carry away—even though signs warn visitors that it is illegal to do so. Each year, my friend told me, the park service in Hawaii receives more than a ton of such stones sent back in individual packages, carefully wrapped by those who purloined them, usually with maps drawn to show just exactly where, please, the stones should be replaced. The letters which accompany those returned rocks usually contain catalogues of the misfortunes which befell those who stole the stones. Even more recently, a friend from the Southwest told me that the same kind of bad luck seems to visit those who take pot shards from the Anasazi sites. There is no doubt in my mind that no good fortune will come to those who break away pieces of Wo-ja-ho-sen.

Ironically, the island of Wo-ja-ho-sen, in the 1970s, was the only portion of the state of Vermont officially registered as the property of the Abenaki people of the state. But that island is not, in spite of its small size, unimportant to the Abenaki. *Wo-ja-ho-sen* means the "Guardian's Rock." Another of its names is Odzihozo, the great transformer hero of the Western Abenaki people, the one who shaped himself out of Earth after some of the dust of the Creation fell from *Tabaldak,* "the Creator's," hands. Long ago, they say, after Odzihozo had almost finished transforming the shape of the world—forming the valleys by dragging his body through them, piling the mountains with his hands, making the long channels for the rivers to flow—he came to this place. It was very beautiful and peaceful here with the great mountains on either side. Today, the mountains to the west are called the Adirondacks, the ones to the east, the Green Mountains. So he worked very hard here and made a big lake, the lake the Abenaki people call *Petonbowk,* "Waters That Lie Between." Then he looked around. He had been busy for a long time. He made the land a good place for those who would come after him. Now it was time for him to rest. And this was the best place to do it, this bay which was so lovely. Thus, he changed himself into stone so he could sit there and enjoy it through the ages. That is how that story ends and does not end. For when the Vermont Abenaki people call that island the "Guardian's Rock," they are not just thinking of the past. Odzihozo is there and he is still alive. And the Abenaki people still visit that island to give tobacco and thanks. They guard Odzihozo as he guards them.

▲▼▲

The office of the Abenaki Self-Help Association in their tribal council building at Swanton is in a building which was once a depot for the Burlington Northern Railroad Company, now leased to the Abenakis for a token amount. The older name for the area where Swanton now stands is *Missisquoi.* Missisquoi, which may be translated as the "Flint Place" or the "Place Where the Waters Circle Back," has been a place of refuge and a settlement of Abenaki people for many centuries, especially since the 1800s when they dropped out of sight. "Keeping a low profile" might have been invented by the Abenakis. (A recent program was done on National Public Radio about the people at Swanton in which they were referred to as the "invisible Indians.") Like Rock Dunder in the midst of the bay, they have remained, yet been seldom recognized by their real names. There were reasons to hide.

△▽△

There is a mountain named Grey Lock. It was once the name of an Abenaki warrior. To keep the land of Missisquoi, he and his men waged a guerrilla campaign as fierce as that of the Vietcong. After each raid he would disappear. No one knew where. In *Ndakinna,* "Our Land," Grey Lock found refuge. And his name and the name of the St. Francis Abenakis (as the people who fled to Canada after the destruction of Norrigwock were now called, that village of refuge holding not just Abenaki but also Mohican and other dispossessed people of the North-east) struck fear along the frontier. Often they had to do little more than to come to the edge of a new settlement and sound the war cry. The white settlers would flee. Many expeditions went into the mountains to find Grey Lock. None of them ever found the old warrior—though he found some of them! Those who pursued Grey Lock learned well the meaning of his Abenaki name—*Wawanolet,* "He Who Throws the Others Off the Trail." It is said that he was over a hundred years of age when he disappeared into the mountains for the last time. It is said by some that he never really died. Like Odzihozo, he has become a part of the earth and is still watching and guarding *Ndakinna.* Those long years of warfare and the threat of Grey Lock and other warriors are one of the reasons that so much of northeastern Vermont remains wild to this day. In yet another irony, the very wildness and beauty made that land desirable during the second half of the twentieth century. Nature sanctuaries, housing developments and private parks began to spring up. They shut the contemporary Abenaki people away from their sacred land, away from the spirit-strengthening power to be felt walking that earth, away from the hunting and fishing and trapping which is still a necessary part of the contemporary Western Abenaki way.

▲▽▲

In October 1759 Rogers's Rangers struck St. Francis. His tactics were those of the massacre raids more than a hundred years later at Sand Creek and the Washita, tactics that would prove standard operating procedure in Vietnam two centuries later. One Abenaki tradition says that the raid came at the time of the Green Corn Festival. Most of the warriors were out of the village. There were few to defend the village from the whites. Only the old, the children, the women.

Rogers estimated he killed two hundred Abenakis. Twenty were taken prisoner, and the town burned. It was, such chroniclers as Francis Parkman said, a necessary action. The Abenakis had been the major troops for the French from 1754 through 1760, the ones who made Ticonderoga (as Parkman put it), "a hornet's nest, pouring out swarms of savages. ..." Yet they were people fighting for their lands, their identity as a people, their survival on their own land.

Abenaki traditions discount Rogers's figures of two hundred killed. They say that like later body counts in Southeast Asia, that number was greatly exaggerated. Some say a Stockbridge Indian in Rogers's forces slipped away and warned the Abenaki ahead of time so that the village was mostly deserted when the Rangers arrived. Accounts vary. Father Roubaud, the French missionary who was then at Odanak, wrote several years later that the population of St. Francis (or Odanak) was five hundred at the time of the attack. Some of the Akwesasne Mohawks say that the Abenakis transformed themselves into birds and animals when the British attacked. Then they made their way down to Akwesasne where they turned themselves back into people and found refuge. To this day, there are many Akwesasne Mohawks who are part Abenaki. Such Mohawk names as Benedict (Panadis) originated with the Abenaki influx. Most of the survivors of the raid, though, either eventually returned to Odanak or went further to the south and east along the shore of Lake Champlain to join relatives and friends at Missisquoi.

In 1766, at a meeting with the governors of New York and Quebec at Isle La Motte, the Abenaki delivered the following words as part of an address: "We the Misiskuoi Indians of the St. Francis or Abenaki Tribe, have inhabited that part of Lake Champlain known by the name of Misiskuoi [since] Time unknown to any of us here present, without being molested or any one's claiming Right to it, to our knowledge. ..." It was not too long after that, after a number of swindles which took away from the Abenakis the title to their traditional lands at Missisquoi, that the people began to follow a two-hundred-year policy of being invisible. They drifted back in small family groups to the area which had once been theirs.

By the early 1700s it was plain to the Western Abenaki, especially those in what is now western Maine, New Hampshire and Vermont, that they had four choices—give up and die, continue to fight as guerrilla warriors, flee or blend in. Most chose the last three alternatives. Wawanolet, as I have mentioned before, waged such a successful guerrilla campaign in northwestern Vermont that he delayed the white encroachment on that part of the Northeast to the point that even today it is thinly settled. From his "castle" near Missisquoi (the present-day Swanton, Vermont), he launched raids south throughout the Green Mountains. The British never defeated him or brought him to the council table. It was largely out of fear of Grey Lock that the British agreed to peace with the Abenaki and left them alone from 1727 to 1744. He was yet another "bad Indian." In other words, a patriot chief. There is no record of his death, and no white man knows where and when he was buried. Some of us simply say that he never died. The current militant chief of the Vermont Abenaki, Homer St. Francis, is a direct descendent of Grey Lock.

Abenaki people fled west and north. Many took refuge among Grey Lock's people in and around Missisquoi. Some went deep into the northern mountains of New Hampshire, Vermont and Canada—where their descendents remain today, many of them "undocumented" as Indians.

Other Abenaki chose to simply blend in. By keeping a low profile, Abenaki villages survived into the twentieth century. In one case, a small village actually existed on the shores of Lake Champlain until World War I. They lived in longhouses and wigwoms (wigwom is the Abenaki word for "house") and existed by hunting, fishing and trading for a few material goods. One night, however, the decision was made by some town fathers to get rid of the "gypsies," who were aliens and might even be German sympathizers and were not to be trusted because they went back and forth between there and Canada. They came down on the Abenaki village with armed men and trucks, loaded the adults into the trucks and gave the children up for adoption. The trucks roared out of town, and no one knows for sure what happened to those people.

By the 1900s it was clear in Vermont that being an Indian was not a wise idea. Most Abenaki (like my grandfather, who lived in the Adirondack foothill town of Greenfield Center) called themselves "French." Even so, in Vermont a "eugenics project" was proposed prior to World War

II. Records were carefully made of all people in the state of "inferior" blood—such as Indians. Had the project been carried out, they would have all been sterilized. As it was, many families suffered from this project. The records of the abandoned eugenics project were only found a few years ago. Ironically, those records turned out to be of real use to the Vermont Abenaki in their attempt to prove (after many years of hiding in plain sight) that they are, indeed, Indians.

It is impossible to summarize even the highlights of a complicated people's complex history. The evidence of the existence of the Abenaki and other related nations can be found throughout New England, as can the people themselves. The name Connecticut is *Kwani tekw.* The "Long River." Many words which are a part of the English language today come from Abenaki, such as moose, canoe, toboggan and moccasin. Yet there are those who denied and still deny the Abenakis their very existence. The founders of the state of Vermont put forth the legend (which is even mentioned in a poem by Hayden Carruth, as if it were gospel) that there were no Indian inhabitants of Vermont. Thus, the land was free for whites to claim it. But the archaeological evidence and the genealogical research show that Vermont was and still is inhabited by Abenaki people. A touchy situation for the lakeshore developers, mountain developers, condo and ski-run owners, being on land that was never legally taken—by sale or treaty—from people who still exist. And it was because of such things as development and the excavating of Abenaki graves (some not that ancient) that the Vermont Abenaki people resurfaced in the 1970s. Inspired by the activism and the successes of the Penobscot, the Vermont Abenaki have pursued a course of nonviolence and direct confrontation to prove their claims to aboriginal rights. Among other things, Homer St. Francis (yet another bad Indian—especially as portrayed by some of the news media in Vermont) had Abenaki license plates made up for his car and ordered the federal government out of the Missisquoi Wildlife Refuge (which was created recently out of land used for thousands of years by the Abenaki for subsistence hunting, fishing and trapping and, perhaps, in ceremonial ways, though again that is something I cannot talk about).

The creation of that wildlife refuge—and the barring of the Abenaki from lands used by them for millennia—is one example of the reasons the Vermont Abenaki chose to make themselves visible again. They hope, too, to better their situation through communal action. "Getting ahead" as an individual really doesn't work for Native Americans. For one, the scales are weighted against them. Four centuries of disease, deceit and prejudice have resulted in the Abenaki people having the lowest per capita income of any group and the highest rate of unemployment. For another, being "Indian" means being ready to share. Following traditional patterns, including the vitally important one of loyalty to family, has meant that Native Americans throughout North America have not fared well in a society where money is more important than loyalty and getting ahead is valued over living in harmony. The Abenaki are no exception. The Abenaki staged "fish-ins," fishing without licenses, in order to bring their cases to court. The first results of that came, in 1989, when a judge ruled that the Abenaki had proved their case. They were, he ruled, descendents of the Abenaki aboriginal inhabitants of Vermont and had the right to fish without licenses. The state of Vermont appealed the case, but it was an important step. I was a very small part of that case, testifying as a storyteller in the trial, citing and telling certain traditional tales with which I have been entrusted to illustrate the relationship of the contemporary Abenaki people of Vermont to *Ndakinna,* "Our Land."

And the bones came together. Today, the Western Abenaki have reappeared. They have stood up and spoken their real names. With their hunting and fishing lands threatened, they have engaged in "fish-ins" like the Indians of the Northwest and have begun to try to educate both their own children and the general public about the Abenaki heritage which is as much a part of the Green Mountain State as its maple sugar and deposits of marble. After so many years of silence, there are some who wonder where they were, who doubt that they are Indians at all. But such ethnologists and historians as Gordon Day and Colin Calloway have concluded that the people of Missisquoi are indeed who they say they are. In the years to come, there will be some rethinking done about the "extinction" of tribal peoples in the Northeast.

Like many other Native American people, I'm a person of mixed blood. My Abenaki ancestry is from my mother's side, my father is Slovak. I'm proud of both sides, and my father sometimes spoke of the similarities, of being treated like a foreigner in your own land as the Slavs were in Europe, of following old ways. But I was raised here in the Dawn Land, the foothills of the Adirondacks, which are named after the Abenaki. An old tradition in the Abenaki language tells how some Iroquois people and some Abenakis met and confronted each other near Saranac Lake. Perhaps it happened thousands of years ago, when the Iroquois were just migrating into the Land of the Dawn, establishing sway over this part of North America so that Lake Champlain was to be the main boundary water between Abenaki and Iroquois. The two parties called each other names. "Maguak," said the Abenaki. "You are people afraid to fight us." That name became Mohawk. "Anentaks," said the Iroquois, observing the Abenakis habit of chewing on spruce gum and pine pith. "You are bark eaters, beavers." That name became Adirondack.

My great-grandparents were Basket Makers. My great-grandfather left Canada and came to Saratoga Springs to the Indian encampment in Congress Park to sell baskets to the tourists. He ended up staying here, living on Cole Hill in Porter Corners on a mountain which has been home to Indians—and to our ancestors' Indian burial grounds—since time immemorial. Just over that mountain was, until just before World War II, a sizeable community of Native Americans living in the valley of the Sacandaga in longhouses and cabins. They had no acknowledged claim to their land and were flooded out by the Sacandaga Reservoir. Today, I am still engaged in a fight to prevent the development of that mountain and the desecration of those hidden burial places.

I write and tell traditional stories which illustrate the ideals of living in balance with the natural world and the people, ideals which were part of Abenaki culture way back when and remain important to this day. They are important lessons—lessons which the Abenaki needed to hear—for they were human beings and prone to make mistakes. The power of Native American traditions does not come from Native Americans being perfect but from those traditions satisfying the deep needs which people have for good guidance. The essays which make up this book are part of my own attempts to express and follow those teachings. Perhaps, also, to help a few others see the value of trying to live in balance, to listen to words which come from the earth, to respect the old stories. Those words and stories have helped me many times. I offer them to others in the hope that they may, perhaps, do the same.

▲▼▲

"The land was ours before we were the land's ..." so said the poet of New England, Robert Frost. But his poem and his vision didn't recognize the Indian—except as a vanishing red. For there were and there are people who not only were owned by the land, but who could, like Odzihozo, disappear again into the earth. Once, when I was much younger and a student in a university, I thought that those who were silent had nothing to say. For a time I forgot the lessons my own grandfather taught me by saying nothing. Now, a bit older and much less wise, I've heard songs which others said had vanished. I have learned there are words and stories which should only be spoken when the time is right. Staying close to the earth (trusting in an older balance than machines and metal of the kind of power which comes and goes with elections) helps us listen and keep some of that silence as we gather the bones together.

References

James Axtell, *The Invasion Within: The Contest of Culture in Colonial North America* (New York: Oxford University Press, 1985).

Colin Calloway, *The Abenaki* (New York: Chelsea House Publishers, 1989).

Colin Calloway, *The Western Abenakis of Vermont, 1600–1800* (Norman: University of Oklahoma Press, 1990).

Richard Carlson, *Rooted like the Ash Trees: New England Indians and the Land* (Naugatuck, CT: Eagle Wing Press, 1987).

William Haviland and Marjorie Powers, *The Original Vermonters: Native Inhabitants, Past and Present* (Hanover, NH: University Press of New England, 1981).

The Wabanakis of Maine and the Maritimes: A Resource Book about Penobscot, Passamaquoddy, Maliseet, Micmac and Abenaki Indians (Bath, ME: American Friends Service Committee, 1989).

Understanding the Great Mystery

✦

In 1992, while visiting Baffin Island to talk with Inuk elders about hunting and its relationship to the balance of all things, an old hunter named Akaka told me a story of an old walrus. That old walrus offered itself to a young hunter as the man paddled his qayak through the ice floes where there were many walrus, trying to decide which animal to strike with his harpoon.

"I want a drink of water," the old walrus said. "Give me a drink of water."

But instead of killing the animal, the hunter laughed at it.

"Your tusks are too dark. You are too thin and old for me to kill."

As soon as the hunter said this, not only the old walrus but all of the other walruses slid from the ice into the sea. None of them came back up, and the hunter went back home empty-handed.

I think of that story often, for it exemplifies so much about the way Native people see the world and interact with that great mysterious force which those raised in European culture call "Nature."

In European thought, Nature and Man are separate. The Old Testament of the Bible, in English translation at least, says that humans have been given dominion over nature. That which is spiritual is often defined as being above or apart from nature. In much of traditional Western thought, the natural world is an adversary, a mindless, spiritless thing to be controlled, subdued and used. This can be seen in virtually all of European literature, past and present, especially the folk and "fairy" stories in which the natural world is a dangerous forest, a desert wilderness where monsters dwell and where the devil holds sway. When Hansel and Gretel are lost in the forest, they find themselves the captives of a cannibalistic witch. In the story of Little Red Riding Hood, a wolf comes out of the forest to eat the little girl's grandmother and threaten the child herself. It is only with the appearance of a woodsman, a person whose livelihood destroys the forest, that the heroine is saved and the wolf killed.

It is only within the last hundred years that the idea of wilderness as a positive thing has crept into European consciousness with the creation of a conservation ethic. The influence of Thoreau is important. But few seem to know that the New England transcendentalist's ideas were shaped not only by Asian thought but also by the American Indian vision of spirit in nature. The link between Thoreau and Native thought has been explored by Professor George Cornell, an Ojibway writer from Michigan. Cornell further develops, in his unpublished Ph.D. thesis, the strong links between the whole idea of a conservation ethic and Native American traditions. That link is not the subject of this essay, so I will only mention it in passing and urge those interested in pursuing it further to seek out Cornell's writing, some of which has appeared in *Akwekon Journal,* a Native American publication.[1]

Let us turn back to that Inuk story and look at the lessons that it teaches, for they are crucial to begin to understand that which cannot be truly understood, that force which permeates all of Creation. That cosmic spiritual force is known by many different names, including *orenda* in the Iroquois language, *manitou* in Anishnabe, *wakan* in Lakota. In the language of my own Abenaki ancestors it is spoken of as *manido* and, sometimes, as *nwaskw.* One of the terms we use to refer to that force, that Creator of all things, is *Ktsi Nwaskw,* "Great Mystery."

In the Native cultures of North America, the work of the traditional hunter is not only vital for the survival of the hunter's family, it is also filled with danger. All life is sacred, and so when a hunter goes out to deliberately take the life of another being, that hunter is doing a very serious thing. One's mind and one's spirit must be in the right relationship or one will fail in hunting. An unprepared hunter might even be injured or killed. Among the Abenaki people, going to hunt for an animal such as a bear might require ceremonial purification in the sweat lodge before setting out. Unlike hunting in the Western world, where hunter and prey are engaged in a purely physical process, in North American Native thought, hunting is a process which involves cooperation between the spirits of hunter and hunted. It is a sacred undertaking. In the pueblos of the Southwest, special songs are often sung to the spirits of deer before going to hunt them, and pollen and bits of turquoise may still be placed in the footprints of deer when tracking them. The spirit of the hunter speaks to the spirit of the hunted animal asking permission to kill it. The necessity of the hunt is explained—not for sport or personal gain, but to help the hunter's people survive by providing them with food and clothing and all the things an animal's body may provide.

If the hunter explains his purpose clearly, then an animal may choose to sacrifice its body, though its spirit will survive. I know a Seneca story in which a hunter shoots an arrow at a bear. That bear allows the arrow to strike it. Then the bear continues on its way, after throwing down a skin bag full of meat. That skin bag full of meat is the bear's physical body, but its spirit continues to survive unchanged by death. However, if the hunter does not treat the body of the animal with respect, the spirit will observe this disrespect, and in the future that hunter will not be successful. Part of the respect may be an exchange of gifts. The animal gives its body to the people, and the hunter may offer something to the animal's spirit. When an Abenaki hunter kills a bear, for example, he may offer tobacco.

In the case of the walrus in the Inuk story, it is said that sea animals such as seals and walruses are thirsty for fresh water. When killing a seal or a walrus, a traditional Inuk hunter melts some snow in his own mouth and allows that water to fall from his own mouth into the mouth of the animal, giving it a drink. When the Inuk hunter in the story refused to accept the great gift offered him by the old walrus, which said it wanted a drink of water, thus indicating its willingness to die, he showed great disrespect. The lessons of this story are many. Our lives are not merely physical, and we cannot measure things by their appearance. Spirit is in all things. We must show respect for all things and accept the gifts of spirit in the proper way. If we fail to do this, then we will suffer.

That lack of understanding of the spiritual nature of all life, of the great mysterious spirit which is in nature and which we must respect, has been at the root of the current environmental crisis which we now face. When we think we own nature, as one might own an article of clothing, we begin to see it as something which we can wear or simply discard when it is no longer useful. When we see nature as a thing, without spirit, then our actions toward nature are seen as having no spiritual consequences.

But the Native way is very different. The stewardship of human beings is not as owners, but as partners with many other beings, such as the animals. The animals are recognized not only as spiritual beings but, in some ways, as beings wiser than humans. Unlike humans, they do not forget the right way to behave. A bear never forgets that it is a bear, yet human beings often forget what a human must do. Humans forget to take care of their families and forget to show respect to other things. They become confused because of material possessions and power.

This potential for confusion was true for Native people long before the coming of Europeans (though Europeans have raised the art of spiritual confusion to a new level!). That is why the traditional teachings remain so important. They remind human beings how to take care. The old stories are one example. One of the most important roles of the old stories is to remind people of the right way to behave. The Cherokee tell the story of *Awi Usdi,* the "Little White Deer," who makes sure that hunters behave properly. If a hunter should kill a mother animal with young ones or kill more animals than are needed, then Little Deer will visit that hunter in the night and inflict him with rheumatism so that he will be too stiff to hunt.

▲▼▲

When hunting is done, as it has been done in the West, for sport or for profit, then no concept of physical or spiritual balance rules the hunter's actions. If there is a certain number of buffalo, then—to a Western hunter—that is the number which can be killed. The result of such market hunting in the nineteenth century was the complete extermination of many populations of animals and birds.

A similar attitude has been taken by Europeans toward the forests of the Americas, seeing them as wilderness to be cleared or as logs to be harvested. Though the concept of the sacred grove existed in ancient Europe, it has not been carried over into the Christian era. But the Native view is quite different. Chan K'in is the spiritual elder of the Lacandon Mayan people of Mexico. The lives of his people depend upon the rain forest, which is shrinking further each year, but Chan K'in, who is well over 110 years old, sees it in larger, more spiritually interconnected terms. "Each time a great tree falls," he says, "a star falls from the sky. Before we cut a tree, we must ask the guardian of that tree. We must ask the guardian of that star." When I spoke with Chan K'in recently, he told me of his fears for all living things if we destroy all the forest. "The great cold and the great dark will come upon us," he says.

Like the animals, the plants have spirits. Throughout North America, whenever plants are harvested, it is done with an awareness of the life and spirit of the plant. To gather medicine plants, for example, one must be in the right frame of mind. "If your spirit is wrong when you go out to gather medicine," an Onondaga elder told me, "then those plants will hide. You won't be able to find them at all." The Iroquois people refer to the primary food plants—Corn, Beans and Squash—as the Three Sisters, those who sustain us. When planting those seeds, working in the gardens and harvesting, there are old songs and ceremonies which honor the spirits of the Corn, the Squash and the Beans. It may be said, quite literally, that there is no difference in Native North America between planting and prayer.

I have often heard it said by Native elders of different nations that "We Indians have no religion." This is a statement made because of the great knowledge which Native people have of Western religion after five hundred years of being proselytized. Native people have been viewed at various times as beings with no spirit, "like animals" (a simile which carries some special irony for Native people), as devil worshippers or as empty spiritual vessels ready to be filled with whatever brand of Christianity is being served up by the missionary of the day—Baptist, Catholic, Protestant, Seventh-Day Adventist or Mormon. A few years back, my friend Powhatan Swift Eagle had a little Native American jewelry shop on Broadway, the main street in Saratoga Springs, New York. As I sat with him one summer afternoon, he was visited by no fewer than five different missionaries, all wanting to convert him from his heathen ways to their *true* religion.

Red Jacket, the great Seneca orator, made a famous response to a member of the Boston Missionary Society at a meeting called in 1805. "Brother," Red Jacket said, after being lectured at length about the follies of Indian paganism, "you say there is but one way to worship and serve the Great Spirit; if there is but one religion, why do you white people differ so much about it?" Red Jacket also showed his own knowledge of Christianity even further by pointing out that, "If you white people murdered 'the Savior,' make it up among yourselves. We had nothing to do with it. If he had come among us, we should have treated him better."

Red Jacket might also have pointed out that the Iroquois and other

Native people did not see the natural world as being evil or at odds with spirituality, but that the presence of *orenda*—the "sacred"—the presence of the Great Spirit is to be found in all things. If religion is defined as something which separates human beings from the plants, the animals, the stones and places them in a position of dominance over or opposition to nature, then "religion" is something which was indeed foreign to the Native peoples of North America. Further, if religion and one's spiritual life is relegated only to what goes on inside a building one day in every seven, then that "religion" was something that Indians neither needed nor wanted. Red Jacket went on to say that he was aware of the fact that the missionary had been preaching to the Christian neighbors of the Senecas. Yet being Christian did not seem to prevent them from mistreatment of the Indians. "We will wait a while," Red Jacket said, "and see what affect your preaching has upon them. If we find that it does them good and makes them more honest and less disposed to cheat Indians, we will then consider again what you said."

The idea of the sacred being everywhere is expressed in many ways by Native people. Long Standing Bear Chief, a Blackfoot elder, published a book called *Ni Kso Ko Wa* in 1992. It explains Blackfoot spirituality and traditions and contains this simple and eloquent statement about sacred places:

> Wherever you are doing something ceremonial, that place becomes sacred. The entire earth and everything about it is sacred, not one place more than the other.[2]

Because of the powerful sacred nature of Creation, then, there is ideally no distance between human beings and the earth. It is said among the Mohawk that the faces of our children not yet born are just there, under the earth. It is also commonly said throughout the continent that the very old and the very young are especially blessed because they have either just come from the earth or are just about to return to the earth. Both ages are very close to the Great Mystery.

When one begins to understand the Great Mystery, to know (in a way which transcends conventional knowing) that our human spirits are part of a great circle of spirit, then that understanding must also translate itself into action. We begin with thanks. An Onondaga elder told me that he reminds himself to be grateful every day for everything he is given. He says a prayer of thanksgiving each time he drinks a glass of water. If we were all to be so thankful and so aware of the powerful, mysterious, spiritual gift which water is, would we not be more likely to keep it clean for future generations? An elderly Mohegan woman named Fidelia Fielding kept, in the early part of this century, a journal in her own language. Some years ago I worked on a translation of her words, and I was moved by their simple eloquence. Each morning she recorded her thanks for simple things, being able to get up from her bed, being able to stand. *M'undu wi go,* she wrote, "The Creator is good." *Ni ya yo.* "It is so."

There is so much to be thankful for and so many gifts which we fail to acknowledge. Yet those simple words of Fidelia Fielding, whose Indian name was Djits Budunacu, "Bird Which Is Flying," offer a good place to begin. With such acknowledgment and thanks we begin to walk a balanced path of caring and caretaking, a path which leads us back into the circle of spirit. And in that circle we may begin to understand the Great Mystery.

Notes

1. George Cornell, "Native Americans and Environmental Thought: Thoreau and the Transcendentalists," *Akwekon Journal,* vol. IX, no. 3 (Fall 1992), 4–13.
2. Long Standing Bear Chief (Harold Grey), *Ni Kso Ko Wa* (Browning, MT: Spirit Talk Press, 1992).

ROOTS OF SURVIVAL

✪

Waudjoset âtlokawâgan biwakamigwi alnôba bimisigeniganiye agwedewâbizun. So a traditional story might be introduced in our language among the Penobscot people. In English translation those words might be approximately translated as follows: "My story is walking around, a forest lodge man whose clothing is made of moss and whose belt is a strip of white ashwood." *Wâwogit âtlokawâgan.* "Here my story lives." It is important to pay attention to that traditional opening, for it makes it quite clear that a story is not just an invented narrative, not just a collection of words. A story is a living being. It is present, not past or passed by. We must understand that to understand what stories mean to Native people.

An understanding of the place, purpose, structure and vitality of traditional stories is also important for anyone who wishes to understand contemporary Native Americans. Traditional tales inform and strengthen our cultures and our people, even those who are not fluent in a Native language. The values exemplified in those old stories, which become new each time they are told, can be found in the work of virtually every Native American author and the words of every Native American storyteller. The strength of those traditions—which are not dying out, even though there have been great changes in Native American life and lives over the past five centuries—and their continued survival have made the roots of contemporary Native writing that much deeper. Even new stories are often told in ways which have been shaped by those old forms, those lasting values, which come from the oral tradition. In retelling those old stories and telling the new ones, we can come to a special understanding about the Indian relationship to the world around us. That relationship, which is rooted as deeply as the tallest trees, has a great deal to do with a vision of time that is different from the Western world's way of chronological perception.

Time

Mink once stole the Sun
so the People could have light.

Then the Europeans came
and brought with them
a new thing called Time.

So Mink stole Time.
He carried it off—
a big metal clock.

But instead of owning it,
he soon found out that
it owned him.

To this day he sits
with three big keys
around his neck.
Each day he uses them
to wind up Time
which owns us all now
the way we once owned the Sun.

Perhaps the best known and most frequently studied Native American novel is N. Scott Momaday's *House Made of Dawn*. It begins with the word *Dypaloh* and ends with the word *Qtsedaba*. Those words, which refer to the "start of the day" and the "day's end," have been used for centuries by Pueblo storytellers to lead into and then out of a story. They set the frame within what might be called "Indian time," a time which has nothing to do with clocks and everything to do with the natural progression of light and dark, of sunrise and sunset—the real, living day. Leslie Silko's widely praised novel *Ceremony* opens and closes with the word "Sunrise," which, I am told, is the first word spoken in ceremonies at Laguna Pueblo, Silko's home community. Sunrise and sunset, not just for one day, but for all days. The same sunrise and sunset seen by our most distant ancestors. A measure of time which is unchanging.

▲▼▲

When, in 1989, I was called into court to testify on behalf of the Abenaki Nation in that "fish-in" trial, I told stories. I chose two traditional tales which are still well known and widely told among the Vermont Abenaki people. They are stories which illustrate the long tenure of the Abenakis in *Ndakinna* and their relationship to the land. The first, which can be found in an earlier essay in this book, tells of the shaping of the area now known as Vermont and the creation of Lake Champlain by Odzihozo as he dragged his body across the ground. That story, I explained, is a very ancient one. It goes back to the time of the glaciers when the land was shaped. It links that timë to this time. What is long ago for European Americans is just yesterday—or still today—for Indians.

The second story told how Azeban, the Raccoon, fell into the falls on the Missisquoi River when he tried to shout louder than the sound of the waterfall, became dizzy and fell into the rapids. You may think you are powerful, but you cannot speak louder than nature. My testimony was given over the objection of state lawyers who tried to characterize such stories as ethnocentric, inaccurate and changing from year to year. The judge, who seemed very interested in those stories, overruled all of the objections of the state lawyers. The stories, I said, were for all human beings. Their purpose was to help people learn how to live in balance with each other and with the earth. They were passed on from generation to generation with great care and their nature was sacred. It was a good day to be a storyteller and to have the stories I told be of use to the people. That case was decided in favor of the Abenaki people, even though it was later overturned by the Vermont Supreme Court. Their basis for overturning the judgment? They agreed that the Abenakis had proven their point, but this had all happened "so long ago" that the weight of history was against the Indians. Two hundred years is too long a time. Yet for Native Americans, two hundred years or even ten thousand years may not be seen as a long time when it is seen through the eyes of the stories that link us to that circle of life which includes our ancestors and the generations as yet unborn.

▲▼▲

Among most, if not all, Native American cultures on this continent, stories were meant to both entertain and teach. In *All My Relations: Sharing Native Values through the Arts,* Ojibway storyteller and writer Lenore Keeshig-Tobias says, "Storytelling is never done for sheer entertainment, for the stories were and are a record of proud Nations confident in their achievement. Stories contain information about tribal values, patterns of the environment and growing seasons, ceremonial or religious detail, social roles, geographical formations, factual and symbolic data, animal and human traits."[1]

▲▼▲

And this all occurs within the Native perception of time. Natural time, not clock time. Perhaps, since "time" is such a Western concept, we might say that there is simply an indifference to its strictures. The Western concept of time is something like a straight line. We walk from the past through the present toward the future. I was once given by one of my Native elders a much different, Indian view of how we travel through our lives. Think of yourself, he said, as walking backwards. What you see most clearly is the past, continually getting larger as we go along. The past is always part of the present. Now and then, perhaps, you may look over your shoulder and get a glimpse of something which is approaching. Some people can do that often and "see into the future." Moreover, that journey you are on is not in a straight line. The path meanders and even circles back.

That different vision leads to the structure of those Native American novels mentioned earlier. *House Made of Dawn* begins in the "present," leaps back into the past, then goes forward, then back and, finally, having made a complete circle, ends at its own beginning. In *Ceremony,* where traditional Laguna stories retold in poetic lines weave in and out of the narrative, the character of Old Grandma remarks at the end of the book, "It seems like I already heard these stories before … only thing is, the names sound different."[2]

Stories are living things. Like all living things, stories are sacred. In *Achimoona,* the Cree writer, Maria Campbell, tells us that the word in her language for the mind is *mom-tune-ay-chi-kun,* a word which means the "sacred place inside." That is the place where we dream, imagine, talk to the grandmothers and grandfathers. The word for expressed thoughts is *mom-tune-ay-chi-kuna,* which is translated as the "wisdoms." These are the thoughts and images from this place which are given to others in the shape of stories, songs, dances and art of all kinds. They are gifts from that sacred place inside.

Whether spoken in a traditional story or written on a page as contemporary poetry or prose, those gifts from the sacred place within are still being offered to the world by our stories. Those gifts, which have helped Native American people survive close to five hundred difficult years of disease, racism, stereotyping and neglect are being offered to all human beings. If accepted and understood, they may help us all to find ourselves in time—not ruled by time or running out of time. In Indian time, in the sacred time of stories, we may find the real roots of survival.

Askwa âtlokawâgan paiâmuk. "My story is still traveling on."

Notes

1. Catharine Verrall, comp., *All My Relations: Sharing Native Values through the Arts* (Toronto, Canada: Canadian Alliance in Solidarity with Native Peoples, 1988).
2. Leslie Marmon Silko, *Ceremony* (New York: Viking Press, 1977).